PRAISE FOR

# *The Healing Game*

As someone who overcame a chronic health condition, I know what it takes to heal the physical body through dealing with emotional trauma. For me, it was a minefield as I sifted my way through a myriad of challenges that I had experienced, unpicking them myself, one by one. In this unique and comprehensive book, Annabel Fisher has provided a road map for that journey. It covers all aspects of the healing process, and gives the reader a road map to heal themselves. It's also a great resource for practitioners to give to their clients, to support the work they do with them. It is the book that I wished I had had when I was healing, and it is set to create a massive wave in the self-healing industry.

**Sasha Allenby**, co-author of *Matrix Reimprinting using EFT*, author of *Write an Evolutionary Self-Help Book*

My guess is, if you are reading this book, you are ready for change. As human beings we tend not to change anything until it becomes too uncomfortable to live with, until the pain is too great, the sadness, anger or fear is too much and we wake up and realise we are missing out on the life we wish to live. NOW is the time to reclaim your life and allow Annabel Fisher to hold your hand and expertly guide you through The Healing Game, helping you move from illness to wellness, from victimhood to empowerment, putting you back in the driver's seat of your own life and enabling you to see and experience the world in a whole new way. Enjoy your journey to wellness.

**Sharon King**, Creator of the Matrix Birth Reimprinting technique and author of the upcoming book, *Heal Your Birth, Heal Your Life: Tools to Transform your Birth Experience and Create a Magical New Beginning,* www.magicalnewbeginnings.com

If you've been suffering from a long-term or serious disease and feel anxious, terrified, confused, disappointed, and you blame your body for letting you down and have tried absolutely everything to no avail . . . this book is for you!

Annabel Fisher is truly one of a kind. An innovative healer, a passionate inspirational speaker and a woman with a huge heart and a huge story. The book you hold in your hands is not your typical healing manual. It is a heartwarming story of a woman struggling to overcome her own illness and in the process discovering what she now calls "The Healing Game".

I have personally worked with Annabel as she helped me heal from a recurrence of breast cancer which is, I am glad to say, now in remission. I have gratefully witnessed her focus, her dedication and her incredible knowledge in EFT and Matrix Reimprinting.

"The Healing Game" makes her process transparent and accessible for others who are also passionate to provide healing against all odds.

I owe you my life, Annabel. Thank you!

**Ingrid Dinter**, Accredited EFT Master Trainer
www.IngridDinter.com

As an EFT Practitioner and Trainer, my clients often say "I just don't know what to work on next!" In this heart-journey book, Annabel gives us a clear structure and a profound, yet simple, recipe to clear out the emotional contributors and limiting beliefs that often lurk underneath the surface of illness. Any reader will be able to help themselves with this valuable 9-element format, to effect ease, grace, relief and healing (emotional and physical) in their lives.

I can't recommend Annabel's book highly enough for anyone who has put themselves last on their own priority list as a matter of course. It's easy to understand, thorough, and fun to work through, even though it covers a serious topic. Her clear message—that illness is an opportunity to heal our inner wounds—offers hope and love to the troubled body-mind and soul.

**Liesel Teversham**
Author of *No Problem: The Upside of Saying No*
www.savvyselfgrowth.com

Annabel Fisher's "The Healing Game" is a gift to anyone whose illness or chronic condition has been a mystery, a trial or a cause for fear or hopelessness. The holistic healing approach she advocates (EFT) has never seemed so accessible or sensible than by her example and through the simplicity of the exercises she encourages. I found myself, an experienced practitioner, hungrily exploring her suggestions and playfully allowing the EFT process to help me anew. Her approach is a distillation of much that is helpful in our field, and I appreciate just how she takes a stand for the quality of self-care, and curiosity that is required for us to finally allow healing in places where it's seemed all but impossible.

**Jade Barbee**, Certified EFT Practitioner and Trainer, AAMET International, www.EmotionalEngine.com

When I first met Annabel, I struggled to believe that the vibrant woman in front of me was the same person I'd heard stories of who couldn't get out of bed. Since then, I've gotten to know Annabel better and I see her as the real deal - a true healer whom I have referred many clients to. I trust her and her work completely. In *The Healing Game*, Annabel guides you in understanding what triggers chronic illness and walks you – with compassion and awareness – through the process of transforming your health.

**Paul Zelizer**, Business Coach for Conscious Entrepreneurs and Co-founder of Wisdompreneurs www.PaulZelizer.com

*The Healing Game* is a must-read for anyone suffering from any chronic, debilitating condition. In a conversational and easy-to-follow format, Annabel shares many invaluable insights not only about the *cause* of chronic pain and suffering, but also practical tools and strategies that can lead to a permanent *cure*. I have experienced the benefits of EFT first-hand, both personally and professionally in my practice, and I have not seen a more comprehensive and helpful resource for anyone wishing to use EFT to assist others, or to reconnect with their innate ability to be well. *The Healing Game* is a healer's gem!

**Dr Christian Guenette**, Chiropractor, co-creator of
*The Thought That Changed My Life Forever*
www.happynessunlimited.com

I promise you that this book will push your buttons. There will be times where you'll want to slam it closed. However, within these pages, Annabel Fisher has given you a clear path to reclaiming your health and vitality. If you're sick and tired of being sick and tired, this book will give you the courage, strength and strategies to heal.

**Dov Baron**, bestselling author, founder of
Full Monty Leadership and one of Inc. Magazine's Top
100 Leadership Speakers, www.FMLeadership.com

In *The Healing Game,* Annabel Fisher helps the reader identify the real triggers, or causes, of illness. She challenges our belief systems and guides us from victimhood into self-awareness and empowerment. Annabel equips us with tools and strategies to transform our attitudes and health. Annabel was once housebound and in a wheelchair. But with Tapping Techniques, she recovered from an 'incurable disease'. Within two years she'd become a well-established EFT Practitioner. Congratulations to Annabel for doing a beautiful job with *The Healing Game* and for all of her work to help others reclaim their health and power.

**Lindsay Kenny**, Founding EFT Master,
www.ProEFT.com

Working as a client with Annabel Fisher has been one of the most deeply meaningful and transformative experiences in my life. Her warmth, intuition, dedication and remarkable talent guided me out of Crohn's Disease and into a vibrant, healthy, and purpose-driven life. Annabel's highly skilled work comes together in a powerful combination in this exciting new book. She shares her wisdom and working knowledge with the same compassion as when I was her client, shedding light on the dark corners of illness and offering insight, hope and a path to healing.

**Sarah Vanderheiden**, Advanced EFT and Matrix
Reimprinting Practitioner

Suffering from chronic pain of a long-term illness? Want to transform your life from illness to wellness? Caring for, or working with clients with chronic pain or disease? Then *The Healing Game* is a must-read book for you. Using EFT, Annabel Fisher builds on her personal knowledge of chronic illness and ten years of practice experience to skilfully teach you the rules of *The Healing Game*. Know the nine rules well and play the healing game to transform your life.

**Dr Elizabeth Boath**, Associate Professor in Health, Staffordshire University, UK. Advanced EFT and Matrix Reimprinting Practitioner and Trainer and Clinical Hypnotherapist

This may be the most important book you will ever read! How much is your health worth to you? As someone who has played *The Healing Game* to overcome chronic pain and debilitating illness, I can testify that it works. You couldn't ask for a more capable guide on your healing journey than Annabel Fisher.

**Eleanore Duyndam**, Executive Producer, *EFT Radio*

People travel internationally to train with Annabel. The attraction is the incredible depth that she brings from her own healing experience. Annabel's book, *The Healing Game*, is a gift of remarkable interventions that are especially tailored for you. Her intuition comes from thousands of clinical hours of working with clients.

**Mary Llewellyn**, EFT Founding Master

Annabel Fisher has written a really valuable and practical book about how to use EFT for chronic illness. Although presented as a 'game', it is a step-by-step guide that contains everything you need to begin using these techniques for your own issues. It also provides a helpful reference that you will be able to go back to in the future. Read *The Healing Game* and you can start using it straight away as a self–help manual.

**Prof. Tony Stewart**, EFT Master Trainer

*The*
# HEALING
# GAME

# *The*
# HEALING
# GAME

## Transforming Chronic Illness
## Using EFT

# ANNABEL FISHER

DIFFERENCE MAKER PRESS
Vancouver, Canada

*This book is for all my clients, past and present.*
*Without your vulnerability and willingness to dive in with me,*
*this book would not exist.*

# CONTENTS

# An Invitation to Transform Your Health

BY EFT Master Karl Dawson

My own journey with Emotional Freedom Techniques (EFT) began with several chronic health conditions. In fact, I was so sick, that at the time, I was being tested for stomach cancer, had a prolapsed disc in my lower back and several other physical issues.

When an acupuncturist first suggested that there might be a link between my physical symptoms and my emotional health, I was surprised, to say the least. In fact, I remember arguing with him and calling him an idiot punctuated by several expletives!

That initial consultation, however confronting, was the beginning of my journey into the understanding of the link between emotional health and physical disease. To cut a long story short, I discovered EFT and my own health transformed dramatically.

I didn't stop there. Not only did I go on to train as an EFT Master with the originator of EFT, Gary Craig, becoming one of only 29 original EFT Masters trained by Gary, but for some years, I also specialised in EFT for serious diseases.

What may seem like miracles to the modern medical paradigm soon became commonplace to me. Time and again I introduced EFT to those who were physically sick. Time and again, they healed. I'm talking about a dramatic reduction or a resolution of conditions such as chronic fatigue syndrome, bipolar affective disorder, fibromyalgia, arthritis, chronic pain and a whole host of conditions that are considered incurable by the Western medical paradigm. I've also seen people turn around the most life-threatening conditions when the medical industry had given them up as terminal.

All of the people that transformed their health had one thing in common – when the underlying emotional causative factor of a physical condition was identified, the body healed accordingly.

I went on to create my own advanced EFT technique, Matrix Reimprinting, and co-authored two books on the technique that were published by Hay House. I have trained over 3,500 Practitioners worldwide – something I continue to do to this day. So not only have I had the pleasure of seeing these health transformations first hand, but the wave has rippled out and the stories of others' healing have become commonplace in my everyday reality.

Recently, I launched my second co-authored book *Transform Your Beliefs, Transform Your Life: EFT Tapping Using Matrix Reimprinting*. At my book launch there were several people that presented who, many years before, were sick with crippling mental and emotional diseases. They thanked me for my help, but in truth, it is the techniques themselves that enabled them to transform disease.

That takes me back to before Matrix Reimprinting was created, when I was specialising in EFT for Serious Diseases. I created and taught a specialist course for practitioners, enabling them to identify and resolve the underlying causative factors that are common in the healing of a health condition – factors such as how our subconscious beliefs can keep us in a state of ill health, how we can have unconscious conflicts that we aren't even aware of, that prevent us from healing, and many other underlying emotional factors that aren't even considered in our current Western healing paradigm.

So it was a great pleasure to hear that Annabel had written this book. The thing that I found, and still find common today, is that by the time a lot of people get to EFT, they have pretty much tried everything else, and have spent a lot of their resources on getting help. They often don't have the money to invest in extensive one-on-one work with a practitioner. What was missing in EFT was a companion book that could help people systematically organise their recovery, and work through the majority of the underlying issues alone.

I'm not saying that this book replaces the need for practitioners completely. In fact, often we cannot see our own blind spots, and it is helpful to have someone else to guide us through. What this book does do is give those who are healing a great resource to uncover and transform their own health challenges. It's a book that those on a budget can use alongside getting other forms of help. It will support the journey to health that anyone who is using EFT on themselves is making. And it is definitely a book that I would recommend to my practitioners worldwide.

If you are holding this book in your hands and just about to embark on a healing journey, I recommend you dive in. If you just read the book, and think it sounds interesting, it is not likely that anything will change. Over the years, and with all the people I have worked with, the real results have come when they consistently dived in with the tapping (however strange it might seem at first), and got to the core of their challenges in this way.

You have in your hands a book that could quite literally transform your emotional health. It may transform your physical health in the process too.

I wish you all the best as you dive in, get tapping and make a change.

**EFT MASTER KARL DAWSON**
Creator of Matrix Reimprinting and co-author of
*Matrix Reimprinting Using EFT* and *Transform Your Beliefs, Transform Your Life: EFT Tapping Using Matrix Reimprinting.*

# The Healing Game

BY ANNABEL FISHER

D ID YOU EVER PLAY *The Game of Life*? A popular board game when I was a teenager growing up in the 80s, it simulates a person's travels through their life, from college to retirement. To succeed at *The Game of Life* you had to collect a number of 'pieces' along the way – jobs, marriages and possible children - all of which were determined by the spin of a wheel.

Healing long-term or chronic illness has some key similarities, as well as some vital differences, to that particular game. However, what I am going to present to you in this book might challenge your assumptions about which parts you have control over and which parts are left to fate.

In the popular Western model of illness and disease it is often assumed that, just like in *The Game of Life*, the spinning wheel comes to a stop, and we subsequently fall prey to some external force that is way beyond our control. If that describes your current belief system, this book is not only going to show you that you are not at the mercy of an external force, but it is also going to show you that it is possible to take back control and transform chronic or long-term illness. You will learn that you have more power to create this transformation in your well-being than you may currently believe.

Where this book is similar to the popular board game is that we are going to go through a process that allows you to collect a number of different 'pieces' along the way. Not necessarily more knowledge, because although we are told that knowledge is power, it is likely that at this stage of your healing, knowing facts about your condition does not necessarily equate to healing it. Instead, what you will find in this book is a specific and unique process that enables you to take action. This process forms the basis of *The Healing Game*, a system that I created after thousands of clinical hours with private clients. It can be applied to any chronic condition with often dramatic results.

Before we go any further, it is important to clarify that I'm not trivializing your current predicament by inviting you to play *The Healing Game*. As someone who has transformed chronic illness myself, and has supported countless clients worldwide to do the same, I am only too aware how alienating such a concept can initially be, to someone who is sick. Your mood today as you read this – whether optimistic about recovery, feeling ground down by the whole process, fed up, bitter, angry or doubting anything can change – will determine how readily you are able to receive this information. I know only too well from my own journey and from being in a situation similar to your present one, that a voice of optimism is not always easily received, especially if you've listened to a number of such voices in the past, and nothing has really changed.

It might take a leap of faith to join me on this journey, but it certainly won't be blind faith – I'm going to share with you tools, techniques and processes, and once you start consistently applying them, they are likely to create some form of transformation in your mental, emotional or physical state straight away. And I'm going to ground these tools in cutting-edge theory around mind-body medicine so that you can really start to see the connection between your mind and body and begin to heal it accordingly.

This is a deep game I'm inviting you to play. To go through this process is going to require you to take a really strong, hard look inside: to identify what was going on in your life when you first got sick, and to help you address any underlying challenges that you may not have faced since. None of this is going to take place at a surface level. We'll be ploughing deep into your subconscious, facing unresolved issues that may be at the heart of your condition or disease, and transforming them accordingly. I'm going to show you how almost everyone that I've worked with, myself included, became ill when they lost touch with their true, authentic self, and I'm going to help you face and rediscover that which you've lost touch with since you became sick. It's *The Healing Game*, so you'll find a light touch all the way through, and I'm going to help you to take the heaviness out of your recovery, but it's definitely not a *Trivial Pursuit* that we will be undertaking together.

I can't promise you that taking this journey is going to heal your condition. What I can promise you is that if you make a dedicated commitment to undertaking this journey with me, *something* is going to dramatically change. Applying the processes in this book is likely to first and foremost change your whole perception about your health and well-being. It's going to put you back in charge of your life. You'll learn to take control of your emotional climate, releasing any stress, fear or shame around your current health challenge. You'll experience more peace around being sick, learning how to be present with where you are now, letting go of longing for your old life back, or worrying about what the future holds. You'll feel less like a victim of your condition and more like someone who is able to consciously take responsibility for their health. And as a side effect, your physiology *may* begin to change. This, as I say, I cannot promise you as, although you will read many case studies in this book from people whose physiology was transformed as a result of playing *The Healing Game*, I see this healing more as a by-product of transforming emotional stress, trauma and subconscious programmes, rather than the sole reason that we will go on this journey together.

So, I invite you, wherever you are on your healing journey right now, to take this leap with me. It isn't something you will be able to do with half your heart. You could read the concepts in this book and think they sound interesting or understand them on an intellectual level. But the real journey begins when you take the leap with me and start consistently applying the process presented in this book and commit to whole-heartedly playing *The Healing Game.*

I look forward to supporting your process. Let the journey begin!

Annabel Fisher

October 2014

# Playing The Game

## My Own Healing Story

*I'll never recover. In fact, I'll be ill for the rest of my life.*

It was the belief that dominated my reality for the majority of the time that I was sick. My body had let me down. Failed me somehow. Broken down to such a point that at times I couldn't see a reason to carry on. Or so I thought back then.

It would be easy for me to transport you into the story of my suffering at that time. To share the pain of being trapped in a body that barely functioned, the desolation of being wheelchair-bound, and the utter and relentless exhaustion that accompanies a period of long-term illness. If you are recovering from chronic illness yourself, you might have a moment of catharsis whilst reading my words. Maybe some of the things that I experienced would mirror your own, and our souls would connect in that place as we shared the experience of human suffering.

I'm not going to meet you in that place. Because from where I sit now, I know that the relief you'd gain in that moment would be temporary. That reassuring moment where you knew you had been met by another being who knows your grief for the time you have lost would be fleeting. You'd put the book down, scan your body, look down at your weary aching limbs, and tell yourself that everything is exactly the same as before. No, I'm not going to meet you in that place.

Where I am going to meet you is somewhere entirely different. Because this story doesn't start when I was sick, housebound and desperate. Neither does it start when I was wracked with pain and wheelchair-bound. Or when my body was so intolerant to so many different foods that I could barely nourish it. Nor does it start when I barely slept, awoken frequently by the intensity of my own nightmares. Instead, this story starts at my turning point.

The learnings that we have in each lifetime come in many forms. Sometimes they come in neat packages that are easy to comprehend and understand. Other times they come in a form that is so incomprehensible that it takes a total paradigm shift to even comprehend them, let alone apply them. Mine was the latter. My answer came in the most unlikely package, and was brought to me by my good friend, Leon.

Just to be clear, it would be easy to read my story from this point and imagine that I just lay in bed until the answer came. The truth is, I felt as though I'd tried almost everything by that point. As many before me had done, who had taken their healing into their own hands because there was little the conventional medical paradigm could offer. I felt I'd tried everything before the day that Leon came.

I'd tried countless approaches with my physical body. I'd had acupuncture. I'd been massaged, which was excruciatingly painful in my physical state at the time. I'd dragged my body through various exercise routines, including bed-yoga and T'ai Chi, both of which were an incredible effort. I'd tried to tackle my challenges on an energetic level, including modalities like Reiki and chakra balancing. I'd spent relentless hours in the counselling chair and at CBT (Cognitive Behavioural Therapy). I'd tried positive affirmations, repeating them over and over again. (Looking back, I'm not sure how much I believed what I was saying. Affirmations can be very useful, but they are unlikely to transform your mental and emotional state alone. They are dealing with the conscious mind, and as you will learn in this book, much of what you are experiencing is happening on a subconscious level.)

My diet was also immaculate – I was gluten-free, caffeine-free, alcohol-free and dairy-free. But I wasn't free! Despite all I'd tried, while there had been some minor relief, I was still sick. I soon sank into a depression with feelings of hopelessness, helplessness, and on more than one occasion, suicidal thoughts. So on the day my friend Leon came to see me, I was at my lowest point.

## THE 'ANSWER'

"I think I have the answer for you," Leon told me, as I opened the front door.

At this point, I was in the 'What have I got to lose?' phase of my illness, so I listened to what he had to say.

What Leon presented to me that day was something totally out of the box! Something so out of the existing medical paradigm of sickness and well-being that it's a wonder that his message even reached me. And so it was, in the unlikely setting of my living room, with his enthusiasm and my reluctance, he presented me with EFT (Emotional Freedom Techniques).

Whether you are new to EFT or a seasoned practitioner, it's pretty universally accepted that, out of all of the therapeutic interventions, it ticks all the boxes when it comes to weirdness. It's hard enough to accept that tapping on acupuncture points whilst verbalising certain statements is going to impact stresses, anxieties or phobias, for example. It can be near enough impossible for a wheelchair-bound and depressed being to comprehend that this strange tool could make the slightest bit of difference to their health. You may be reading this book through a similar filter, barely entertaining that what it has to offer may be of the slightest bit of help.

I'm guessing that for every enthusiastic EFT practitioner like Leon who reaches out in this way, maybe one in ten weary and desperate souls respond. Probably because, as it was with me, there is the sense that there is nothing left to lose. I'm happy to have been in that minority. One of the aims of this book is to raise the odds so that sceptics can make the decision to jump, based on the many case studies of others who have done the same, and not just based on a whim, because, frankly, they are out of hope or options. But there was no book like this to bridge the gap back then for me.

I had a profound turning point that day. I knew deep within me that I would heal. There was no doubt in my mind. I went from hopelessness to seeing that healing could be possible. It also shaped my career path and my destiny, bringing me in line with my true purpose and enabling me to gobally reach a multitude of people. You could say I am extremely grateful to Leon for what transpired on that day.

## BEYOND FEAR

When Leon asked me what I was feeling at that time, I told him I was afraid. There was the fear that I'd never recover. Fear that I would be trapped in this cycle of disease for the rest of my life. Fear that this was all I would ever be. I was angry, lost and afraid. Leon saw all this and more.

In a conventional therapeutic setting, a practitioner might have brought this fear to the surface and helped me face it. We would have got it out of the box, talked about it, looked at it from different angles, perhaps tried to shift my perception about it in some way. At best, a therapist might have been able to temporarily pacify me so that I would be more willing to submit to my situation. Perhaps even find a glimmer of peace in the suffering. Thankfully this was not a conventional therapeutic situation.

I believe that although there is obvious value and sometimes catharsis when we discuss our challenges in the conventional way, the *feeling* usually remains the same, even when the perspective changes.

What happened in this session was the polar opposite. We used the EFT Tapping Protocol to get right to the heart of my greatest fear – the fear that I'd always be this way. It wasn't actually the thought that I would never heal that was the problem. When we have a thought or belief such as this, the emotional disturbance is caused by the underlying *feeling* that accompanies the thought. It was this underlying feeling, along with all the accompanying fear, anger and despair, that Leon helped me resolve that day.

It literally felt like someone had removed the part of my brain where those feelings were being generated – no matter how hard I tried - and believe me, I wanted to prove him wrong! - I couldn't access that part. Of course, I could still think the thought that I'd never heal, but it didn't have the same impact anymore. Instead, what I did feel was hope. Not a false hope born from misplaced positive thinking, but an unshakable knowing that I would fully recover. And that hope replaced the pain and doubt that I had been feeling up until that moment. And so, the *real* journey to healing began.

## THE BODY AS THE MESSENGER

With Leon's help and my own reawakened enthusiasm, I began to understand the link between my inner emotional state and my physical condition. It wasn't simply the beliefs that I could never heal that we addressed with EFT, but rather how the emotions created by my life experiences were influencing my present physical state. I began to see how my body was not the enemy that had failed and deserted me, but rather how it was a powerful messenger that created feedback between my perceptions, my experiences and my external world. My unresolved emotional challenges had thrown my body out of sync, and my body bore the burden. And as I faced these challenges, and the unresolved accompanying emotions one by one, releasing their charge and transforming them with EFT, my body began to heal accordingly.

## FROM PUSHING TO PEACE

At first I overdid it.

It's understandable. Not only was it part of my make-up to push in order to achieve, but I was hungry for resolution. The same fierce tension that had driven me to sickness also drove me to work on my own healing. But soon I began to relax into a rhythm that was more supportive to a healing journey. In other words, I stopped fighting the illness, surrendered, and addressed my challenges from that place (all of which I am going to support you to do in this book).

One of the key things that I did which set me apart from some of the other people that practiced EFT, is that I rarely, if ever, used EFT to focus on the symptoms. I understood instinctively that the symptoms were not the problem, and I focused on the emotional drivers. When I did this, the symptoms took care of themselves, because they were only the *indicator* that something was wrong. The real healing took place when I was able to really go beneath the surface of them and reveal what they were actually about. That is when my body began to change.

Within a few months I was walking with a cane, or with the support of someone's arm, and five months later I was training to be an EFT practitioner. Within 18 months, and with careful management, my symptoms had disappeared entirely.

## GOING DEEPER

The emotional drivers that I addressed went much deeper than the fear that my body would never heal: a complex web of related beliefs, shaped from my earlier life experiences, plus the current environment that I had created for myself, had contributed to my physical breakdown.

I had always believed that people who rested were weak, and this belief had not allowed me to give way to illness for some time. But I also had an unconscious conflict where I yearned to be nurtured and cared for because I didn't have this need fulfilled in my marriage – the illness was a perfect creation within which this need could be met. Also, what it meant was I no longer had to continuously take care of others, which was something that I'd done for as long as I could remember as a serial people pleaser. Because up until that point in my life, never knowing how to say no and always putting others before myself was a standard for me.

There were also the various roles I'd been playing that reflected my people-pleasing ways, especially in my marriage, where I'd swallowed down my feelings of isolation and a lack of fulfilment for so long that it had manifested in chronic illness (in my case, chronic fatigue syndrome (CFS)). All these challenges I addressed and transformed with EFT.

Hungry to share what I had learnt with others, I soon trained as a practitioner, helping clients from all over the globe to create physical transformation through addressing their underlying emotional drivers. Two years later I was training practitioners. There are now EFT trainers all over the world who do amazing work. But people travel internationally to train with me because what I offer is enmeshed with the depth that my own healing experience brought. Not superficial tapping scripts which scratch the surface of physical challenges, but deep interventions tailored to each individual to really take the lid off the emotional components of a physical illness. And out of many thousands of clinical hours of working with clients and training practitioners, *The Healing Game* was born.

## YOU AND THE GAME

I am often asked for the one thing that I would share with those who are recovering from illness or disease. It's simple. Illness offers us the opportunity to reconnect with ourselves, make ourselves as much a priority as we make everyone else, and honour our own needs.

I invite you to prepare yourself for a journey that will allow you to do just that. Perhaps there's a voice inside you telling you that I just don't understand what you're going through, and you just can't do that because of x, y or z. I want to invite you to honour that voice, and at the same time, know that you can move beyond it. And the rest of this book will show you how.

# CHAPTER ONE

# Introducing
# *The Healing Game* Process

### How to Play the Game

I INVITE YOU TO PLAY a game with me.

It's one that is probably like no other you have played in your life so far. There are no other competitors and you cannot lose the game – if you play along wholeheartedly.

I cannot promise that you'll always love the game! There will be moments where, just as when you were a child and you found yourself confronted by a certain aspect of a game that felt bigger than you were, you might want to run away. There may be times when the game will make you want to hide, even from yourself. When you will shut the lid on the imaginary box that contains the game and declare that it's just not for you. Perhaps a few days will pass. But the game will call you back. It will call you back because you have a yearning inside you. A calling to be well, and it's one you can no longer ignore. And so while this game might shake you to the core, I want you to know that I am right here with you. I'm the other player: your companion in this game, not your competitor. Because I wholeheartedly want what you want. I want you to be well. And while you play this game, I am beside you all the way, cheering for you, rooting for you, and just plain holding a space for you to transform your health, even on the days you doubt that you can.

## WHAT IS *THE HEALING GAME*?

*The Healing Game* explores how many of us become ill when we lose connection with our true, or authentic, self. Your authentic self is who you truly are, beyond your patterns and your programming that have all come from your life experiences. Even while in the womb, you started to learn certain limiting beliefs about how safe and loved you were, which you absorbed from the environment around you. Each time you integrated a belief, you forgot a part of yourself. In this book, you will regain that connection through self-inquiry, transformation techniques and practices. You'll learn to not only identify the conditions that had a role in your current health challenge, but how to transform these underlying conditions through playing *The Healing Game.*

Whether your healing journey so far has been a heavy regimen or a pressured routine, or whether you've been operating from the opposite end of the scale and feeling so overwhelmed that you haven't known where to start, *The Healing Game* will have something for you.

## HOW TO PLAY THE GAME

The aim of the game is to identify and overcome three interrelated challenges that have shown up in all the clients that I have worked with who are recovering from chronic illness. They were my challenges, too. These three challenges form the main components of *The Healing Game.*

They are:

1. The Trigger
2. The Connector
3. The Transformer

Each of these parts contains three further specific components, so that there are nine life areas that we will address in total as we go through this book. We'll break each one down briefly in this chapter and then later on, we'll look at how they apply to your own condition and give you tools to address it: tools that you can self-apply, which have the potential to create transformation in your well-being on a multitude of levels.

## Introducing the Three Main Parts of *The Healing Game*

### PART A: THE TRIGGER

Part A of *The Healing Game* considers what may have triggered your illness. If you are viewing your condition through the conventional medical model, you might be tempted to say something like 'It's my genes' or 'It just happened'. In my experience, I've yet to meet or work with someone who didn't have some kind of trigger that occurred on the run-up to their condition, and we will explore the science behind this later on in the book.

The trigger can be a single event, such as a life trauma, but for many people it is often a series of events that caused a pile-on effect, which eventually showed up in the body as illness or disease.

Just to be clear, it doesn't mean that every time you have a traumatic event or a series of life challenges you will get sick. Much of the outcome of whether these life challenges affect your physiology will depend on a number of interrelated factors, which we will explore as we go through this book. But a key point to note is that for the majority of people who are recovering, there was something in their lives on the run-up to the appearance of their symptoms that created a physical breakdown.

THE TRIGGER will teach you about the contributing factors to your illness, taking you out of victim mode and putting you back in the driver's seat. Some might say that insights aren't enough to heal us, and although there are a number of other components involved in *The Healing Game*, self-insight is one of the first steps to self-healing. As soon as you start to gain insight about the underlying triggers to your condition, self-compassion often begins to emerge. And when you are able to experience self-compassion and release any feelings of self-blame or loathing, it in turn creates a much more conducive environment for physical transformation.

THE TRIGGER is broken down into several sections, which form the first components of *The Healing Game*.

1. Symptoms
2. Satisfaction
3. Showing Up

## Component 1: Symptoms

It doesn't actually matter what symptoms you are experiencing, as *The Healing Game* is not aimed at addressing the physiological symptoms, but rather at the underlying contributing factors to a condition. So this process can be used on any condition, regardless of what is actually showing up in the physiology.

## Component 2: Satisfaction

If you have been ill for some time, chances are your level of satisfaction about your life may be rather compromised. This is something we will help you to transform as we go through this book. But we'll also examine your level of life satisfaction on the run-up to the condition. Not that I'm saying that purposeful and content people never get sick, but a lack of purpose and a general dissatisfaction about life in general can be a contributing factor to a breaking down of the body. Many people that I have worked with were either ignoring their purpose before they got sick or settled for a lesser version of their dreams. Others, like myself, discovered that illness was a wake-up call by which they found their purpose.

## Component 3: Showing Up

In the third component of THE TRIGGER, we will explore how you were showing up in the world when you became sick. This one can be quite challenging to face because it can feel really personal, yet how you are relating to the world can have a profound effect on your physical health.

For example, if you were showing up as what is termed a Type A personality, i.e., you were highly motivated but running the belief that you weren't accomplishing all that you could, you may have felt as though you were constantly burning out and chasing your tail. This could have been a major contributing factor to the breakdown of your body. Similarly, if you were a people pleaser who was consistently putting others first and never saying no, you could have burnt yourself out in a different way.

As we go through this book, we will examine how you were showing up in the world, and the impact that this was having on your health. We'll also address the underlying beliefs that were driving the way that you were relating to your external reality and transform them accordingly.

## PART B: THE CONNECTOR

In Part B, THE CONNECTOR, we explore how we often become sick when we disconnect from our true, authentic self. Sometimes we play out a preconceived idea of who we think we should be. It creates an inner division within us between the role that we play and the call of our true, authentic self. In short, many of us stuff down our truth in favour of either playing a role that no longer serves us, or conforming to our programming or the status quo. THE CONNECTOR examines this tendency and helps us to reclaim our authentic connection. It is also divided into several sections, which create components 4 to 6 of *The Healing Game*:

4. The Gateway
5. Why Can't I . . .?
6. What Would Happen If . . .?

## Component 4: The Gateway

THE GATEWAY helps you to truly remember who you are, beyond the conditions, programmes and beliefs about who you should actually be. We are going to help you reconnect with your true, authentic self, something that you may not have done since childhood, and in the case of some clients that I've worked with, something that you may have never done in this lifetime.

## Component 5: Why can't I . . . ?

In this component we look at the question of why you may have believed, prior to getting sick, that you couldn't live as your authentic self all of the time. We examine both your thoughts and the conditions of your external reality that may have caused you to choose to live from a place of compromise rather than from a place of joy. We'll examine any belief that has prevented you from knowing that you deserve the best from life, and resolve that accordingly. Whether you are operating from the belief that it's not right to live with abundance, or have inherited messages that cause you to play small in the world, we'll look at them and transform them in this section.

## Component 6: What would happen if . . . ?

Next for the curve ball! What would happen if you were to live as your authentic self all of the time? If you haven't been living your truth, a whole variety of justifications for compromising are likely to come to mind. You might even find yourself defending your current point of view or justifying the various roles you have been playing with people. There might even be an element of believing that I don't understand your predicament or challenge. It takes courage to move beyond the preconceived idea of who you think you should be, remove your mask and live your truth, and in this section of the book, we will be doing just that.

In this section we will build a complete profile of the true you, including your gifts (undiscovered or otherwise), your talents, and what fills you with joy. We will begin to build a visual of what your life looks like when you are completely connected, and when you live your life from a place where you feel most on fire with life.

## PART C: THE TRANSFORMER

In the third part of the book we look at what action you need to take in your external reality in order to create the optimum conditions for healing. Just as when a dieter wants to lose weight and does their inner work, but then has to adjust their diet and exercise plans and other aspects of their environment to support their goal, in this section we look at what needs to take place so that you can support your healing process.

I have encountered a number of clients who do not want to change their lifestyle when they have fallen ill, and they expect different results without creating changes.

Whilst the first two components are mostly comprised of inner work, this third component will comprise the changes that need to occur in your world.

THE TRANSFORMER consists of several sections, which form components 7 to 9 of *The Healing Game*.

7. Addressing the Fear
8. Surrendering
9. Taking Action

## Component 7: Addressing the Fear

To those who are well and have never been chronically ill, the idea that there may be any fear around healing may be a confusing one. Yet when we are chronically ill, not only does our perception become distorted in the face of the illness, but there are often a host of accompanying fears to address about what it actually means to return to the world.

Sometimes the illness can be subconsciously protecting us from a life circumstance that we dread returning to. For example, we hated our job, and the illness was a way out. There is no judgement in this and it usually takes place on a subconscious level. But fears such as these are addressed in this section so that our internal world and our external reality align.

## Component 8: Surrender

When I use the term surrender, many of my clients initially become uncomfortable. They misunderstand and think I mean giving in to the illness and subsequently, giving up. But for me, surrender is something entirely different.

For those that consider themselves to be on some kind of spiritual path, particularly a path that contains some form of ancient wisdom teachings, surrender, in one form or another, is usually the central teaching.

You could define surrender, in the context of your healing journey, as a total acceptance of the physical condition you find yourself in. I'm not talking about paying lip service to acceptance whilst internally you are screaming the opposite: "No, this isn't right, this shouldn't be happening to me," but rather total surrender to what is. When you are able to surrender to the condition, you can create healing from that place. When you fight it, the opposite effect occurs and more stress is created in the body.

## Component 9: Taking Action

The final component of *The Healing Game* is about taking action in your external reality to ensure that your external world is lined up with the shift that has taken place in your internal reality. It might mean forging a new career path that you can return to as your body heals; it might mean walking away from old relationships that are no longer serving you, or making lifestyle changes that support your inner world. There may be some initial resistance to making these changes or some 'friction' as you create them, but with the fear out of your way, and with your new experience of surrender, you can make these changes from a place of peace, and begin to create in your outer world the match for the shift in your inner reality.

## WHAT YOU WILL NEED

You won't need any special equipment to play *The Healing Game*. However, I do recommend that you go out and buy a journal or special book in which you can record the exercises. If this is one that divides into sections, even better. Ideally if you have one with separate sections for each of the nine components of *The Healing Game*, you will be able to more efficiently organise the work we do together and track your progress more easily.

## SUMMARY OF THE HEALING GAME

Each of the components has a chapter to itself, so that we can address it in depth as it relates to your life at present. On the next page is a brief summary of the detailed journey that we are about to undertake with *The Healing Game* as we progress through this book.

# The Three Components

**PART A:
THE TRIGGER**

**SYMPTOMS**
What was happening in your
life on the run-up to the appearance
of the symptoms?

**SATISFACTION**
How satisfied were you with your life
when the symptoms appeared?

**SHOWING UP**
How were you showing up in your life
on the run-up to the appearance
of the symptoms?

**PART B:
THE CONNECTOR**

**THE GATEWAY**
Who are you beyond your
triggers, beliefs and programmes?

**WHY CAN'T I . . .?**
What's been preventing you from showing
up in your life as your true, authentic self?

**WHAT WOULD HAPPEN IF . . .?**
What would your life be like if you
showed up as your true, authentic
self all of the time?

**PART C:
THE TRANSFORMER**

**ADDRESSING
THE FEAR**
What fears do you have about healing?

**SURRENDERING**
What would it take for you to fully accept the
condition you find yourself in?

**TAKING ACTION**
What action do you need to take in your
external world to create the ideal
conditions for healing?

Now that we have outlined the basic components of *The Healing Game*, in the next chapter we are going to explore the role that EFT plays in *The Healing Game*, and the dramatic effect it can have on healing the underlying emotional causative factors of your condition. You will learn how to self-utilise it to support you through a profound experience of this process.

# CHAPTER TWO

# Introducing Emotional Freedom Techniques (EFT)

WHEN YOU HEAR THE NAME 'Emotional Freedom Techniques', what kind of image does it conjure up?

When you hear 'emotional freedom', it would be easy to assume that I am suggesting you free yourself of all emotions. If you are anything like I was, there may have been times in your life when you felt your emotions to be a burden and secretly wished to be rid of them. Many people are initially drawn to Emotional Freedom Techniques with this fantasy in mind – that the technique will help them somehow rid themselves of the ups and downs of the human experience. However, this technique is not about dehumanising us or transforming us so that we only experience one single, tranquil mood all the time. Instead, it is about helping us to develop a deeply healthy relationship with our emotional climate. Emotional freedom, in this case, means the freedom from being ruled by your emotions.

Up until the point I discovered EFT, I always felt at the mercy of my emotions. Something that I perceived as 'good' happened in my external reality and my emotional state was correspondingly positive. Someone said something to me that I perceived as a judgement or criticism, and my emotional state plunged into distress. You may have danced this same dance yourself throughout your life, and if so, it is often accompanied by the sense of being at the mercy of the dramas of life. In fact, it is so socially acceptable to have our strings pulled by our external reality in this way that, until I discovered EFT, I had normalised this type of triggering – as have the large majority of people in the Western world today.

One of the challenges with being in a constant state of flux is that, on a very basic level, it impacts our overall health. Stress rises and the levels of cortisol in the body go up, affecting the immune system, as well as a host of other systems in the body, including wound healing, gastric and renal secretions and insulin levels. In short, stress throws the entire system out of balance, and chronic stress can be a precursor to all manner of diseases.

In Chapter 4 we will explore much more deeply how the underlying symptoms of your physical condition can relate to stressful and traumatic life events, but first we are going to learn more about EFT and how to self-apply it.

## INTRODUCING EFT

Have you ever noticed what happens in your body when you experience something stressful or traumatic? It might be your mind that processes the event, but it often shows up in your physiology: a racing heart when you are anxious, a churning stomach when you are fearful, a tension in your throat when you are afraid to express yourself clearly. Whatever it is, there is often a thought *and* a feeling combined. Some of these responses are a natural part of the human condition: a sinking in the chest at a separation, grief in the heart at the loss of a loved one, butterflies in the stomach at the anticipation of a future event. These responses are part of the rich tapestry of being human.

However, there is a deeper level on which we experience emotions, and this is the level on which our response was conditioned by our earlier life experiences. In these cases, we may experience an extreme or prolonged reaction to an external trigger. This reaction is programmed from an experience that has gone before.

## YOUR BODY IS NOT YOUR ENEMY

The retriggering of events that went before is not your body working against you. In fact, it is actually your subconscious trying to protect you from the reoccurrence of similar events. For example, you were shouted at by a man

with a red beard, and it created a rush of fear and humiliation. The next time you see a man with a red beard, the
rush of the information around what happened last time is
re-experienced as a warning from the subconscious to try
and protect you from it happening again. It's often more
practical than we realise. Except it doesn't feel practical
when the trigger occurs. It actually feels very personal,
because we experience it so intensely on the visceral level
and we feel it as though it is real.

The beauty of EFT is that you can release the charge
from a traumatic memory, allowing your subconscious
mind to heal from its reaction to external stimuli. Going
back to the example of the man with the red beard, you
can use the EFT Tapping Protocol to release all traces of
such a traumatic event from your system. This includes any
physical traces (what you felt), auditory traces (what you
heard), and visual traces (what you saw). It can also include
gustatory traces (what you tasted) and olfactory traces (what
you smelt). All these sensual elements are stored in the
body-mind when a traumatic event is experienced, and it
is *these* experiences that are relived in the body when the
traumatic event is retriggered.


## HOW EFT WORKS

EFT involves tapping with the fingers on acupressure
points of the body, while at the same time verbalising a

specific statement about the emotional or sensory symptom that you are experiencing in your physical body. As you tap on the acupressure points and verbalise the specific statement, the body and mind are engaged simultaneously. This releases the energetic charge that is being held by the body-mind, in relation to the particular symptom you are experiencing. Once the energetic charge is released, you no longer experience the trigger.

Identifying where the information is being held in the body and releasing it by tapping on the acupressure points is at the heart of the success of EFT. If you just tap on the statement, but don't marry it with what is happening in your body, you miss a vital part of the process.

Essentially, when we tap, we are communicating with the amygdala – the part of the brain that decides whether or not something is a threat and if it is, subsequently engages the fight or flight response. Tapping sends a message to the amygdala that we are safe. This means that the issue we are tapping on is disengaged from the body's stress response. This can have immediate results, meaning the amygdala no longer sends a signal to the body's HPA (hypothalamus, pituitary, adrenal) axis and we are taken out of the fight or flight response. (We will explore this in depth in Chapter 4.) Tapping also reduces levels of the stress hormone, cortisol, in the body, and is thought to increase levels of the neurotransmitter, serotonin, which contributes to feelings of happiness and well-being.

In addition, it soothes the nervous system, taking it out of a sympathetic response (stress-based), and into a para-sympathetic response (slowing of the heart rate, an increase in intestinal and glandular activity, and relaxation of the sphincter muscles in the gastrointestinal tract).

## HOW EFT CAME ABOUT

Like many of the most effective tools that are on the market today, EFT originated out of an intuitive understanding of the way that the body works.

The EFT story began with Roger Callaghan who had a hit of intuition around a patient he was treating: this led him to originate the tool from which EFT emerged, called Thought Field Therapy (TFT).

TFT came from Callaghan's dilemma of how to treat a water phobic patient. Despite his vast array of skills, the patient that he was treating continued to experience her water phobia. In a eureka moment, Callaghan – a practitioner of acupuncture – made the connection between the anxiety that his patient was feeling in her stomach about the water phobia, and an acupuncture point under the eye. In Traditional Chinese Medicine, each organ has an energetic pathway, known as a meridian, and Callaghan knew that the point under the eye related to the stomach meridian, where his client was feeling her anxiety. Tapping on the point under the eye whilst his client focused on her water phobia, meant that the symptoms abated immediately and she even rushed out to the pool to test the results!

In this moment TFT was born. Callaghan created a host of these tapping sequences, known as algorithms, for a multitude of conditions. There was a certain order in which each acupuncture point needed to be tapped to enable healing for each specific condition.

One of Callaghan's students, Gary Craig, became fascinated by the possibility of making TFT more accessible to a worldwide audience. The challenge he found with TFT was that you had to learn the algorithms for each specific condition in order to get a result. And what about if there were no algorithms for your particular condition? What did you do then? These questions inspired Craig to start experimenting. He asked himself: "What would happen if I collapsed all the tapping points into one single algorithm that could be used on any condition?" He tested his ideas out on thousands of people, and with outstanding results. Over a million people worldwide downloaded the original EFT manual, and millions more have used this technique worldwide to release the emotional charge from their physiology, and experience healing as a result.

If you are just discovering EFT, you are doing so at a time when it is beginning to be embraced by the National Health Service in the UK, and where numerous peer reviews and studies are beginning to emerge.

But for many, this technique brought results as of the 1980s and afterwards, before the scientific research was there to back the simple truth. This technique, despite its bizarre appearance and nature, actually works.

## ISN'T IT JUST THE PLACEBO EFFECT?

In case you have been asking yourself the same question that countless newcomers to EFT ask – namely, "Isn't it just the fact that you believe in it that makes it work?" – I want to highlight to you that it isn't the placebo effect at work when EFT gets results. How do we know? Well, for the placebo effect to actually work, the participant actually has to believe in it. For many people, EFT brings the opposite response when they first encounter it. Sceptics, cynics, doubters and questioners alike have experienced results with EFT.

This is important for you to know on your healing journey, because I suspect that if you have tried a whole host of things, as I did, you may have reached a point where you have given up on anything working. I've had many clients who have felt the same. They often come to me as a last resort when they've tried just about everything else, but somewhere deep in their hearts they have found the courage to keep searching.

So, even if you have a healthy or guarded scepticism, I invite you to dive into practicing EFT on yourself. The key is to fully engage in the tapping exercises. Be present to the feelings that you experience in your body. Show up and engage in the tapping process. The results will speak for themselves if you do, and your scepticism will likely transform into hope and relief.

## WHY WE DON'T USE TAPPING SCRIPTS

EFT is a technique that has grown in popularity, reaching a wider global audience and empowering more and more people to take responsibility for their emotional climate. The downside of this, as with any technique that becomes popularised, is that there has been some watering down of the process. One example of this is the use of tapping scripts.

The challenge that I have with tapping scripts is that they are too general and non-specific to the user. The way that you will learn to work with EFT from this book is to bring it back to what is showing up in your body on an emotional level, and work with that. So, whilst tapping scripts might be a useful way for a newcomer to access EFT, they do not provide the depth with which I am going to be teaching you to use EFT on yourself in this book. The way that we will work is to increase your self-awareness of the underlying emotional charge and release it with the EFT process.

# CHAPTER THREE

# Using EFT On Yourself

I N THIS FIRST EXERCISE, we are going to use EFT on a past memory. To start with, we'll just pick one incident from your past that still has an emotional charge to it. Later on in the book we will look at how to work on a whole memory, breaking it down into different aspects (all the parts of the memory that contain a trigger for you) such as the tone of someone's voice, a look on their face, the contact of their hand on your skin, the smell of the environment, and so on. All these elements can form the various aspects of the triggers that you are still subconsciously reacting to in the present day.

For this first exercise, I invite you to pick a memory from your past that has just one single trigger. A good place to start would be with something that happened in the very recent past, such as a car cutting you off in traffic yesterday, something that someone recently said that was hurtful to you, or something in the news that made you feel sad or angry.

We want to start with something simple: a single event that has one main trigger. When you are choosing this single event, choose an incident with someone who isn't a relative, as relationships with families, because of their ongoing nature, often have a multitude of triggers.

You are now ready to practice the EFT Tapping Protocol on yourself.

---

### EFT QUICK START

Bring to mind the past memory (a single event with a single trigger) that you want to work on.

**Step One – Identify the Feeling and its Location**
What are you feeling and where are you feeling it in your body?
The feeling can be an emotion, such as sadness, fear, isolation, panic, rage, embarrassment, terror, and so on.
The feeling also usually shows up somewhere in the body, for example, the stomach, the heart, the chest, and so on.

**Step Two – Give it a Score Out of Ten**
Once you have determined what you are feeling and where you are feeling it in your body, it's time to give it a 'SUDs' level. In EFT, SUDs stands for 'Subjective Unit of

Distress'. It's the scale that is used to measure how intense the issue is for you in the current moment – 1 being barely there at all and 10 being overwhelming. The reason you take this measurement at the start is that it helps you to see your progress when you apply the EFT Tapping Protocol. The thing to remember about the SUDs level is that it is how you feel in the current moment when you think about it, and not how you felt at the time.

## Step Three – The Set-Up Phrase

The feeling and its location are used to form the set-up statement.

'Even though I have this _____ (feeling) in my _____ (location), I deeply and completely accept myself.'

For example, 'Even though I have this rage in my heart, I deeply and completely accept myself.'

As an alternative to 'I deeply and completely accept myself,' you can use one of the following to create the latter half of your set-up statement:

· 'I accept all of me.'

· 'I accept who I am and how I'm feeling.'

· 'I want to accept myself.'

· 'I'm open to the possibility I could accept myself.'

Tapping on the side of either one of your hands, using the fingertips of your opposite hand, say the set-up statement out loud three times.

**Step Four – The Reminder Phrase**

Now shorten the set-up statement to a reminder phrase. The reminder phrase is what you are feeling and where you are feeling it in your body.

For example: This rage in my heart.

**Step Five – The Tapping Protocol**

Repeat the reminder phrase each time you tap on the following points with your first two fingers, on either side of the body:

- **Top of your head** – right on the crown
- **Eyebrow** – where your eyebrow starts
- **Side of the eye** – on the eye socket bone, at outside of each eye
- **Under your eye** – on the eye socket bone, an inch under the pupil
- **Under your nose** – in the dent which is above your lip
- **Chin** – on the crease of your chin
- **On the collarbone** – if you go out diagonally an inch from where a gentleman would have his tie knot, there is a slight hollow there
- **Under the arm** – for the gentleman, in line with the nipple and for the lady, in line with the bra strap

# Tapping Points

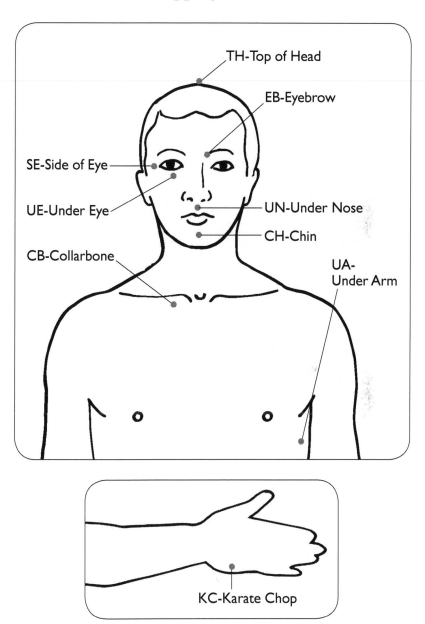

**Step Six – Repeat Several Rounds**

Practice tapping on the points for 3 or 4 rounds so that you get used to them, while repeating your reminder phrase. (Later you will learn to vary the reminder phrase, but at this stage say the same one over and over again, to keep it simple.)

**Step Seven – Recheck the SUDs Level (Score Out of 10)**

Now check if anything has changed. Does the original trigger have the same impact on you? Has the SUDs level gone down? If it has, then great, you have had your first experience of using EFT on yourself. If you didn't get a result or it went up, don't be discouraged. You may have picked a memory that has more than one aspect (such as the tone of your teacher's voice and the look on their face as they scolded you, for example). Later on we will learn how to deal with a memory that has more than one aspect.

You may want to practice working on a few similar memories until you get the hang of the technique. We are going to be doing two things simultaneously as we work through this book. You will be learning how to:

1. Deal with triggers when they arise so that you don't feel at the mercy of your emotions anymore.

2. Clear the underlying emotional memories that are causing the triggers in the first place.

Some of this work will depend on you actually getting triggered in real life! This can be more challenging (especially as you are learning the protocol), because sometimes when we are triggered, we become so lost in the sensation of the experience that we forget we can actually help ourselves. This is partly because triggering can often take us into 'survival mode' which means that we literally operate from the reptilian part of our brain (the part that developed when we were reptiles and lived purely on instinct) instead of the pre-frontal cortex (the part that has evolved with our consciousness). With practice, you will begin to remember to use the EFT Tapping Protocol whenever you feel an uncomfortable emotion arising or are triggered into a survival response.

## EXERCISE

Make a note on a piece of card on how to form a set-up statement.

*Even though I have this* _____ *(feeling) in my* _____ *(location), I deeply and completely accept myself.*

Also note how to form a reminder phrase (the shortened version of the set-up phrase).

From here on in, EVERY TIME you experience a trigger, apply the EFT Tapping Protocol and note the effect it has upon you. You will learn more about why this is so crucial in the chapter that follows.

### Seven Points About Your EFT Practice

1. You can use either hand.
2. You can tap on either side of the body (or both at once).
3. Tap each of the points about 5-7 times. There is no need to count, and it is fine if you tap more or less.
4. It doesn't matter if you miss points out or do them in a different order.
5. If it is difficult for you to say 'I deeply and completely accept myself,' at this stage, try saying something like 'I'm open to the possibility that I can accept myself.'
6. Once you have learnt the tapping sequence, you may find that you get better results by closing your eyes.
7. The SUDs level may go up before it goes down. This is a normal part of the process and doesn't mean that EFT is not working. Sometimes when you feel an emotion that you haven't been in touch with, it heightens before it resolves. (This can be because some other aspect of the memory has come up that is asking to be dealt with. We will address this further, later on in the book.)

Now that you know how to use EFT on yourself, and you have practiced doing so, we are going to fully immerse ourselves in the 9 different components of *The Healing Game*.

# THE TRIGGER

# CHAPTER FOUR

# Component 1
# SYMPTOMS

WHEN YOU GOT SICK, chances are, one of the first things you did was blame your body for letting you down. It's a common response that I have seen in many clients, and one that I couldn't easily let go of myself.

However, one of the most empowering things for you to understand is that the symptoms that you are experiencing don't necessarily mean that your body is working against you, but rather, they are a signal to you that an underlying challenge needs to be addressed so that healing can take place. In this chapter we'll explore the many different messages that your symptoms contain, before taking a look at how to treat them at their source, using EFT.

The first component of *The Healing Game* is identifying the trigger of the condition. This is where the investigative process of *The Healing Game* starts. In the two chapters following this one, we'll look at your life satisfaction when the condition began, and also take a look at how you were showing up in your life when you first got sick. But first, we'll explore your symptoms, how they correlate with the disease process, and how to work with them using EFT.

## GOING DEEPER ON STRESS AND DISEASE

The way that stress contributes to disease in the body is well documented. Your body is actually designed to experience stress and react to it. Some stress can be useful, enabling us to stay alert to specific dangers. Stress becomes harmful, however, when a person faces continuous or ongoing challenges and has no relief in between those challenges.

When there is no relief from stress, we become distressed. Symptoms can include:
 · Headaches
 · Stomach upsets
 · An increase in blood pressure
 · An increase in cholesterol
 · Food intolerances/sensitivities
 · Sleep disturbances

Research from a variety of sources also suggests that extreme distress can bring on or worsen certain disease symptoms. It is estimated that between 75-90% of patients visit the doctor because of stress-related conditions.

Another challenge is that many people self-medicate with alcohol, tobacco or drugs to try to relieve their stress. These three substances actually keep the body in a state of stress, rather than relieve it, so the problem is often compounded.

However, even though the mainstream approach to health and wellness contains an awareness that stress has a major impact on our health, and can be one of the biggest causative factors to disease, we often don't translate this into how we operate in our everyday lives as we ride the rollercoaster of our external triggers. The normalisation of our ups and downs also means, for many of us, a resignation to the highs and lows that they bring. If you've been riding that rollercoaster yourself, I am going to show you how to break that cycle. But first, I want to take a deeper look at why certain life events trigger you into emotional stressors, before we explore how to get resolution on those life events, using EFT. This will enable you to create a more stable emotional climate that supports your physical healing.

## OUR PROGRAMMING AND STRESS

Have you ever wondered why you can experience something that pushes a button inside of you, and the same experience doesn't push a button in your neighbour or friend? Perhaps you found yourself going through something that was incredibly traumatic to you, and the person next to you didn't so much as flinch. The socially acceptable explanation for this is usually something along the lines of: 'I can't help it, it's just the way I am,' but if we go much deeper we can look at not only why specific experiences have programmed you to be triggered in a certain way, but how you can get beyond those triggers with EFT.

## Small-t and Big-T
## Traumatic Life Events

### SMALL-T TRAUMA

There are two categories of traumatic life events that can contribute to a physical health condition. The first we can categorise as 'small-t' traumas. These are the life events that might not seem overly significant. On the grand scheme of things, you might not even consider these events to be traumas. They are the events that gave you certain messages about life. The ones where, in the moment they occurred, you made a certain decision about life that meant that a belief was formed. In other words, the way you subconsciously processed the event led you to a certain conclusion or rule about life that you still live by to this day.

These beliefs create the filters through which you perceive your reality, and they shape how you think, behave and show up in the world. These can include beliefs around your worthiness, loveability, or sense of safety, for example.

As you work through the exercises in this book, the beliefs that you formed in these moments will not only become clearer to you, but you will also learn how they relate to your current state of health. Beyond this awareness, I will also show you, using EFT, how to transform those beliefs and remove the filters that are preventing you from living a full and healthy life.

## THE FIRST SIX YEARS

Of particular significance in the formation of beliefs and their relationship to our health, is the first six years of life. In *The Biology of Belief*, cell biologist Dr Bruce Lipton highlights how, in these first six years, our brains are in delta and theta brainwave states – the same states that hypnotherapists drop us into to make us more suggestible. During this time, we literally download the messages from our environment as if they were the truth. This also includes any messages that we get while we are in the womb.

### *James* – PAIN AND ANXIETY

James came to me with chronic pain and social anxiety. When we started working together, he revealed that he hadn't been wanted. His mother had actually thrown herself down the stairs in an attempt to abort him. James had always had a sense of not being wanted; he learnt what his mother had done in his early teens. His belief was: 'I'm not supposed to be here'. Once we had cleared this belief using EFT, he had more mobility and 50 per cent reduction in his joint pain. He was also able to carry out a presentation in front of his co-workers – something that he definitely would not have been able to do previously.

### *Anne* – Crohn's Disease

Not long after she was born, Anne's father was diagnosed with multiple sclerosis. There was a lot of fear and stress in the family around her father's condition, and early on, Anne learnt that 'The world is a scary place'. Outwardly, Anne always acted as though she was strong, but inwardly, she was terrified. She said she was always 'Waiting for the other shoe to drop'.

Her family didn't talk about her father's condition. She developed an underlying fear and constantly told herself, 'That could be me'.

We used EFT to reframe the belief that her ill health was a self-fulfilling prophecy. We also addressed how she was continuously bracing herself, and expecting the worst. She became accepting of her current situation and released her fears that she would never heal. She is now symptom-free.

## BELIEFS AND BIOLOGY

Dr Lipton also highlights the effect this has on our biology, debunking the significance that the standard medical model places on the links between genes and health. Through his research on epigenetics, Dr Lipton asserts that beliefs switch the expression of certain genes on and off, and that the environment plays a much greater role in our health than our conventional medical model suggests.

This puts the power back into your hands if you previously thought you were a victim of a genetic condition, as Dr Lipton highlights that only a very small percentage of physical conditions are solely gene-related: the rest are a result of the interplay between genes and the environment. My clients will often say something such as, 'All the women in my family have gut issues, that's why I have gut issues', or 'My mother had diabetes, so it's not surprising I have it', or 'My grandfather was diagnosed with MS when he was in his early forties too.'

When you understand that beliefs play such an important role in switching the genes on and off, it means that you can start to resolve any underlying beliefs around your condition.

What this means for you, as you play *The Healing Game*, is that when you resolve the underlying core beliefs that have been created by your life experiences, this not only changes the way that you show up in the world, but it can also create transformation at the cellular level.

## BIG-T TRAUMA

Besides the seemingly small events that shaped your perceptions of life, there are also the more conventional traumatic events that can have a huge impact on your physical health. These are the more classically recognised forms of trauma – in other words, significant life events that can create massive shock and overload in the body, and seriously impact your perception of reality.

There are several key understandings that are not widely understood about the way that big-T trauma impacts physical health, and knowing about them will have a significant impact on the healing of your condition.

Two come from a diagnostic system called Meta-Medicine (which was born out of a similar system known as New German Medicine). These systems correlate the links between stress and disease.

The study of Meta-Medicine and how traumatic events relate to disease is a whole book in itself. But for the purpose of this book, there are some key principles of this diagnostic tool that will help you play *The Healing Game* more effectively.

The first is the understanding that for a traumatic event to create a disease it has to have four elements in place. These four elements, which form what is known as a 'conflict shock', are:

· Unexpected
· Dramatic
· Isolating
· No strategy

They form the acronym UDIN. The 'unexpected' element is a traumatic event that comes out of the blue: you hadn't anticipated it, and couldn't have perceived it could happen. If you had already thought about it or imagined it before the event, then it wouldn't be classed as unexpected.

The 'dramatic' element is a traumatic event with high emotional impact.

The 'isolating' element indicates that when you experienced the traumatic event, you felt alone in the world. You may have literally had the feeling of being on an island when the event happened. If there were other people that experienced the event with you (that were not the perpetrators of the trauma), then it wouldn't impact the system in the same way.

The 'no strategy' element means that you had not developed a strategy to deal with what happened. You may have experienced the freeze response (which we will talk about further in a moment), or been mentally void of the solution to your challenge.

If these four elements were simultaneously experienced, then the incident is much more likely to have created a physical change that the body adapted as a strategy to cope with the information that it could not process.

## *Gillian* – Fibromyalgia

Gillian was in her late fifties and could barely walk without support. She had fibromyalgia, chronic fatigue syndrome, emphysema and chronic pain. She mostly slept upright. The doctors said there was nothing more that they could do.

In our first session, we addressed the general emotional pain she'd felt as a child, using EFT. After this session, she had some limited movement. By the second session, she could tap the top of her own head. We addressed two specific moments that had a dramatic impact upon her when she was young. The first was her father leaving the family home without explanation. The second was his return, a few years later, also without explanation. When we addressed these core memories, and took the emotional charge out of them with EFT, by the fourth session she was walking upstairs, sleeping horizontally in her bed, and had reduced her painkillers by half.

## SYMPTOMS APPEAR IN THE HEALING PHASE

The second understanding that we learn from Meta-Medicine that is relevant to you as you play *The Healing Game* is that symptoms appear in the healing phase of the condition. When we experience a big-T traumatic event (or a series of traumatic events), this throws the body into stress. In the stress phase we have a reduced appetite (because the blood from our digestive system goes to our arms and legs to enable us to run from, or fight, the perceived threat). We often feel like we are 'wired' at this time and sleep is usually also disrupted.

When we perceive that the threat is over, this is when the body is able to rest. It is in this period that the physical symptoms appear. So, contrary to Western medical models, if you are experiencing symptoms now, you are in the healing phase of your condition. This can be tremendously empowering for you to know, because it means that through this model, you can understand that your body is not working against you, and you can work to resolve the perceptions that were formed in the stress phase. You will be able to support your body to heal from symptoms by addressing their underlying causes.

## WHY WE DON'T JUST TAP ON SYMPTOMS

This leads us to understand why we don't just tap on the symptoms in *The Healing Game*. In the current Western medical paradigm, the symptoms are seen as the problem. There is a plethora of pills we can take to mask the symptoms of the condition. With *The Healing Game*, we are not masking symptoms, but rather going to their source.

For this very same reason, we do not need to tap on them. You may find other EFT resources that encourage you to tap on symptoms, for example:

'Even though I have this pain in my lower back . . .'

or

'Even though I have this searing stomach pain . . .'

This can be effective and create relief in some cases. I definitely encourage you to use it in the moment that you are feeling symptoms if it offers you relief. However, I am more interested in helping you find the underlying emotional causative factor that contributed to the physical symptom. Just like taking a pill will only treat the symptom but not the underlying cause, tapping on symptoms will only scratch the surface of the underlying problem.

On my own healing journey, I didn't tap on physical symptoms. I went deep into my life challenges: the frustration and the way I felt unacknowledged in my job, the lack of fulfilment in my marriage, the desperation at not living my life purpose, and the sense that there had to be more to life than this. I tapped on the emotional intensity that accompanied these challenges, and my symptoms took care of themselves. If you have been practicing EFT and only tapping on your symptoms, this will explain why any relief that you experienced may have been temporary. We are aiming for a much deeper experience as we play *The Healing Game*.

## FIGHT, FLIGHT AND FREEZE RESPONSES

Most people are familiar with fight or flight. There may have been incidents in your life where you were triggered and found yourself responding verbally or physically. It is a form of self-protection when you respond in this way. Equally, there may have been times when you experienced a trigger and the best option for you was to run. This is also your survival mechanism kicking in. In addition, there is a third component to the fight or flight response which is less widely understood, but which can have a significant impact on your healing. It is the freeze response.

You may have experienced a traumatic event and felt that there was some kind of weakness or fault in you that led you to freeze. It is actually a primal survival mechanism that is being triggered. Its purpose is simple. An animal in the wild often has a greater chance of survival if it freezes, causing its predator to lose interest and go away. The reptilian part of the brain replicates this when you can't flee or fight.

When a trauma is so significant that it has caused us to freeze, the information is encapsulated, or 'splits off', so that it doesn't overwhelm the body. This becomes problematic when something in our external reality reminds us of when we froze previously. The information that was encapsulated is retriggered and we live the event over and over again. And when the information is retriggered, we experience it as though it is happening in the present moment. This is because the subconscious mind has no time frame. Unlike the conscious mind, it does not know the difference between now and 30 years ago.

## *Anna* – Post-Traumatic Stress Disorder (PTSD) and Chronic Pain.

Anna was one of my workshop participants in Mexico. She'd been in a car crash. In fact, whilst I was working on another student about a car crash, it triggered Anna's memory and she abreacted (she went back into the memory as if it was actually happening right then – a common occurrence in PTSD). Anna had her hands in front of her face, and was screaming. We tapped on all aspects of the collision – what she heard, saw, felt and smelt. After we had cleared all the emotional charge from the memory, she was able to move her body freely for the first time in years. The look on her face is something I will never forget. She told me, 'Finally, I feel free.'

Try this with me now. Think of a situation where you were embarrassed. Nothing too shocking. One where you experienced a significant reddening of the face or racing of the heart. Notice what happens in your physiology when you do. You may find yourself re-experiencing the symptoms. Now, if you have been through something much more shocking than this, particularly when the freeze response was activated, the reliving of the event can be much more traumatic to the body. In the most extreme cases, such as in PTSD, you may re-experience the event with great severity. But even in cases where PTSD is not being experienced, the retriggering of a frozen memory can still cause significant physiological stress to the body and a rush of emotional and biochemical information.

## TRAUMA RELEASE

There is another deeper reason why, as human beings, trauma has an effect on our physiology. In *The Body Bears the Burden*, Dr Robert Scaer highlights how, when animals in the wild experience a trauma, their bodies shake to release it afterwards. Some tribal cultures also do the same. But both humans, and domesticated animals who live around humans, have lost the ability to release trauma in this way. In fact, did you ever start shaking after you experienced a traumatic event? Chances are someone made you a cup of tea, rubbed your back and told you to calm down!

Actually, when we shake, we release the information about the trauma, including the freeze response, from the physiology. If we don't do this, the information continues to be held by the physiology. This is where EFT comes in. Shortly, we are going to be looking at how to release the freeze response from the body with EFT.

⁓ REFLECTION POINT ⁓

· What was going on in your life when you
  started noticing the symptoms or when you
  were diagnosed?
· Were there any life challenges, traumas or
  challenging circumstances that had a cumulative
  effect on the run-up to your condition?

These can either be a series of small events or a major
event.

We often assume something highly significant must
have happened. For me, it was a series of small events
which accumulated: ongoing emotional and physical
stressors at work, a heated discussion with my boss,
feeling unseen in my marriage, a general sense of being
unfulfilled in my life. All this, followed by the sudden
death of my aunt. These stressors (and more importantly,
the way I was perceiving them) combined to create a
tipping point for my condition.

## *Jennifer* - CHRONIC FATIGUE SYNDROME

Jennifer was a social worker. She had a high-pressure
career, and worked long hours with lots of overtime. She
loved her work but was not given emotional or physical
support in her job or at home. She started to feel run down,

dragging herself into work and spending entire weekends in bed. This spiralling finally led her to be diagnosed with chronic fatigue syndrome.

## Working on the Whole Memory,
## The 'Tell the Story' Technique

Now that you already know how to clear a single trigger with EFT, we are going to go deeper and help you to clear a whole memory. It is vital at this stage that you only tackle memories that are emotionally manageable to you. There are a number of reasons why this is the case.

Sometimes you may think a traumatic memory isn't such a big deal, but when you start tapping, it can bring a lot of emotions to the surface.

At other times, you won't be able to access traumatic memories on your own, because the triggers that they contain may have the potential to be so overwhelming to you, that your subconscious will keep you dissociated from them, in order to protect you from the information they contain.

In both these cases, it is advisable to work with a practitioner.

One important thing here: often EFT doesn't work because we start too globally or we pick an event that is part of a series of related memories. For example, I felt unseen in my marriage. There were hundreds of moments when I felt I wasn't seen. If I just picked one and worked on it, I might not get the full relief I was seeking because there might still be a charge from all the other times when I didn't feel seen. Similarly, you are unlikely to get results if you choose an event such as moving house, which may seem like a single event, but actually spans days, weeks or months.

If you have a memory that you feel able to work with and handle on your own, make sure it is a small-t trauma and a single event. By this I mean something that stands alone, rather than something that you experienced multiple times in your life. It needs to be something that happened in a short space of time such as a few minutes. If it spans an hour, a morning, several days or weeks, break it up into a number of smaller events, all with their own beginning, middle and end.

### Step One – The Title

Give the memory you have chosen a title, such as 'The Worst Day of My Life'. The reason that we give it a title is that we can take the SUDs level (the score out of 10) on what emotions the title evokes in you, and take some of the charge out of the memory generally before we get into the specific aspects.

### Step Two – Adapting the Set-Up Phrase

Now create the set-up phrase. This time we are going to adapt it to fit the exercise:

'Even though I have this _____ (feeling + location) when I think of _____ (title), I deeply and completely accept myself.'

Example: 'Even though I have this fear in my heart when I think of The Worst Day of My Life, I deeply and completely accept myself.'

Tap on the karate chop point and repeat 3 times.

### Step Three – Reminder Phrase

Now start to tap around the points. This time you can mix your reminder phrase up a little bit so that you aren't saying the same thing every time. For example:

- **Tapping on the top of the head** – this fear in my heart
- **Tapping on the eyebrow** – the worst day of my life
- **Tapping on the side of the eye** – this fear in my heart
- **Tapping under your eye** – it was the worst day I ever had
- **Tapping under your nose** – this fear
- **Tapping on the chin** – the worst day
- **Tapping on the collarbone** – this fear in my heart
- **Tapping under the arm** – the worst day of my life

Continue until the SUDs on the title is down to a 3 or less (you may not clear it all the first time you use this technique, as aspects that occur later in the story may need to be dealt with before the title is a zero).

## Step Four – Tell the Story Out Loud

Now, start telling the story to yourself *out loud*. You are going to need to be very self-aware at this stage, because the second that an aspect of the story raises your emotional intensity, you are going to tap on it using the EFT Tapping Protocol. We are literally breaking the story down into one trigger at a time. Look for what you:

- Saw
- Heard
- Felt
- Smelt
- Tasted

Each one of these could be a separate trigger.

## Step Five – Tap on Each Trigger Individually

At each point you come to a trigger, adapt the set-up statement to fit the experience, and tap on it until the SUDs level is a zero. Here are some examples of adapted set-up statements for the different senses:

Set-Up Phrase: 'Even though she looked so angry and it gives me this sinking feeling in my chest, I deeply and completely accept myself.'

(Reminder Phrases – alternating between: she looked so angry / this sinking feeling in my chest)

Set-Up Phrase: 'Even though I can still hear him yelling, and I have a ringing in my ears, I deeply and completely accept myself.'

(Reminder Phrases – alternating between: his yelling/ this ringing in my ears)

Set-Up Phrase: 'Even though she slapped me, and it makes my throat tighten with sadness, I deeply and completely accept myself.'

(Reminder Phrases – alternating between: slapped me/this tightening throat/this sadness in my throat)

Set-Up Phrase: 'Even though I can still smell the burning, and it fills my heart with fear, I deeply and completely accept myself.'

(Reminder Phrases – alternating between: the smell of burning/this fear in my heart)

Set-Up Phrase: 'Even though I can still taste the fumes, and it causes a gagging in my throat, I deeply and completely accept myself.'

(**Reminder Phrases - alternating between:** tasting the fumes/this gagging in my throat)

Continue through the memory, clearing each trigger until it is a zero.

### Step Six – Retell the Story Out Loud

At the end, test the original title, and see if there is any charge remaining. Then tell the story again, to check that you have resolved all the aspects. There may be parts that you missed that you need to go back over until the whole memory is a zero.

## THINGS TO NOTE

Even if your story only spans several seconds, it could have multiple triggers. Someone could have walked into the room and told you something and even though that might only seem like one aspect, their tone of voice and the way they looked at you could have been separate triggers, for example. You will need to be really vigilant, particularly to what you saw, felt and heard.

## PERCEPTUAL SHIFTS

At this stage you may notice that the thoughts you had about the memory, before you carried out the tapping sequence, have changed. These are known as perceptual shifts. Often, when you have cleared the emotional charge and the triggers from a memory, you will find yourself thinking something along the lines of: 'I can move on now,' 'It's over,' or 'It wasn't personal after all.' You may find that you naturally reach a place of forgiveness, for yourself or others, rather than trying to force it or feign it (something that you might have tried to do previously and found yourself in conflict with).

## EXERCISE

**First identify all the issues that you experienced on the run-up to getting sick.**

### Part 1 – The Tabletop

In EFT, we use the tabletop analogy. The issue that we are dealing with is the tabletop and all the aspects are the legs of the table (it can have more than four legs!).

These tabletops can include (but are not exclusive to) the following:

- Relationship breakdowns
- Accidents
- Grief or loss
- Unemployment and redundancy
- Family or other conflicts

Make a diagram of your tabletop with all the different aspects (table legs) that are relevant to you (see page 61).

**Part 2 – The Clearing**

Carry out the 'Tell the Story' technique for all your traumatic memories on the run-up to you getting sick. That is, you will use 'Tell the Story' on every table leg you identify.

Only tackle the ones on your own that you feel equipped to tackle.

This will likely take more than one session and this could mean several weeks' worth of self-work as you work through each memory in turn. The key is to do it regularly and consistently.

∞

Make each one into a separate movie. The reason I suggest you do this is that it gives you a clear sense of beginning, middle and end, which makes the tapping more manageable.

Now that you have begun to explore what was taking place for you on the run-up to getting sick, and you have begun to resolve some of the underlying emotional triggers using EFT and the 'Tell the Story' technique, in the next chapter we will explore *Component 2*: your life satisfaction, and take a look at just how satisfied you were with your life at the time you became unwell.

# Tabletop Analogy

RELATIONSHIP BREAKDOWN

Argument #1

Argument #2

Look on their face when they told me

The day they left

First evening on my own

Telling my parents

# CHAPTER FIVE

# Component 2
# SATISFACTION

How SATISFIED ARE YOU with your current life situation?

If you are healing, chances are that this question brings up anything from resentment to despair. Perhaps you have reached a state of optimism by this point, but for many of the clients I work with, that optimism is often for a future moment that will be better than this one, once the body is healed, and not usually for right now.

Chances are, if you have been ill for some time, your level of satisfaction about your life is probably pretty compromised, and understandably so.

But we want to go much deeper than how the illness has left you feeling. Because examining your level of life satisfaction on the run-up to the condition can provide vital clues for underlying causative factors to your current state. As I mentioned in the introduction, purposeful and content people still get sick, just as people can drag their heels in their life situation for decades, and this has no detrimental effect on their health. But a lack of purpose and a dissatisfaction about life in general can be a contributing factor to the breaking down of the body. The lack of healing endorphins in the body when you are in a state of life dissatisfaction can be one explanation. Ignoring your purpose before you got sick, or settling for a lesser version of your dreams can be a trigger to ill health.

## *Donna* – Chronic Back and Hip Pain, Multiple Surgeries

Donna had always wanted to be an artist. She gave way to family pressures and instead became an accountant. She was exhausted and unfulfilled. Although the money she made offered her a good lifestyle, she was not able to enjoy it because she was a workaholic. The chronic pain that she experienced gave her time out from work.

### ∞ Reflection Point ∞

What was your level of life satisfaction when you became sick? On a scale of one to ten, one being completely unsatisfied and ten being totally satisfied, where would you gauge your satisfaction levels on the run-up to your condition?

When I ask clients this question, one of the first responses is often: 'What's this got to do with my being sick?' The challenge is, squashing down how we feel, in favour of carrying out our perceived duty or being a useful member of society, is such a socially acceptable norm that we often don't question it. The whole concept of duty and obligation is heavy for us. And it is heavy for a reason. Often our very soul resists what our mind sets out to do. We find ourselves in conflict between what we perceive we need to do to conform and survive, and our heart's desire to live our dreams and our purpose.

---

### ∽ REFLECTION POINT ∽

Have you ever seen anyone on fire with their life purpose? If you have, what do their eyes look like? What is their energy like? Their demeanour?

How about someone who has resigned themselves to a lesser version of their dreams? What do you notice about the spark in their eyes? What is their general energy like? How do you feel when they are around? What is the external expression of their inner compromise?

---

If you are tuned into the subtleties of the difference between someone living their purpose and someone compromising their dreams, you will know from the outside what that looks like.

And now for the big question: Have you been compromising on your own joy and passion, or living a version of your life that is less than you dreamed?

If you have, this could be having a detrimental effect on your well-being.

### *Christine* – ULCERATIVE COLITIS

Christine had to leave behind a community, friends, support network and family because her husband changed jobs. She began to feel isolated. Her sense of self-worth began to diminish, and she was unsure of her own capabilities.

With EFT, we were able to identify and clear events that had caused her underlying lack of self-worth. She started to acknowledge her accomplishments outside of her marriage. As her sense of personal fulfilment grew, her condition improved.

Just in case you are wondering, this part of *The Healing Game* is not about having everything in perfect order in your life! That's a whole other issue: wanting to have perfect control and have everything 'just so'. But there is a marked difference between those who know what their purpose and their dreams are, and are steadily pursuing them whilst still appreciating what they have, and those that have totally given up on everything other than existing.

So, this first question is designed to help you examine how satisfied with life you were at the time that you got sick. Were you compromising on your dreams? Were you in a state of apathy or dissatisfaction? Were you skipping through your day or crawling through it? Were you living on purpose?

## YOUR LIFE PURPOSE

A deeper part of this question is, did you know what your life purpose was at that time and were you on track with it?

Your purpose is the fire that ignites your life. Without a purpose, you can find yourself drifting aimlessly through life with a sense of emptiness and a lack of fulfilment. Your purpose is the force that can make you bounce out of bed to embrace the day ahead. Compare that to dragging yourself out from under the covers for another day of bill paying. Be honest with yourself about where you sat on that scale when you first became sick.

Some of my clients (as I did) discovered their purpose when they became sick. The illness was the fire that fuelled a different career path – often one in the transformation or health and wellness industries. Others became sick because they ignored their purpose, the repression of their dreams eventually taking its toll.

In Chapter 7, *The Gateway*, we are going to build a complete profile of what your life looks like when you are living in total satisfaction – something you may or may not have experienced in this lifetime. But before that, we want to take a deeper look at why you may have compromised your dreams.

## The Big Why

With this work we are going much deeper than analysing what your life was like and telling you that it should somehow have been different. There is zero judgement of you if, like many of the people around you, you were ignoring your dreams. But we also need to address, beyond your social conditioning, why you may have been choosing to compromise your happiness. There are three main reasons that this would occur:

### UNWORTHINESS

The first reason is that you may have felt a lack of worthiness to live a full and joyful life. It is unlikely that you just woke up one day feeling unworthy. As we said previously, it was your early conditioning, particularly in the first six years, and then mirrored later on in life, that programmed you to feel this way.

### *Tracy* – ADRENAL FATIGUE AND
### MULTIPLE CHEMICAL SENSITIVITIES

Tracy had been physically abused by her stepfather. In fact, he had almost drowned her. She had run away from home when she was a child.

We used EFT persistently to clear her traumatic memories. (In a case such as Tracy's, it is vital that work of this nature be carried out by a practitioner.) We took the charge out of the memories, and Tracy found a sense of self-acceptance as we did so. She began to focus on what she had to offer to the world, taking her focus away from what she perceived was wrong with her. Her fatigue began to subside in the process, as she was no longer in fight or flight all the time.

## PROCESS FOR CLEARING UNWORTHINESS

First of all, identify out of 100 per cent, how much unworthiness you are feeling in your life right now, with 100 per cent being 'I am feeling totally unworthy' and 1 per cent being 'It is barely affecting me at all.'

This percentage level is known as the Validity of Cognition Level in EFT (VOC level for short). It is different to the SUDs level in that it is a way of measuring issues that you are working on over a longer period of time. Each time you clear a memory related to unworthiness, you are likely to experience a drop in the VOC level. You may need to clear a multitude of memories before the level becomes a zero. It is usual that a number of memories have contributed to your sense of unworthiness.

However, if I asked you to identify all the experiences in your life that had left you feeling unworthy, particularly those in the first six years, you may hit a blank. So, we are going to adapt an exercise from an advanced EFT technique called Matrix Reimprinting, from Karl Dawson and Sasha Allenby's book, *Matrix Reimprinting Using EFT*. The exercise is called 'Following the Energy', and is a great way to lead you back to memories on a particular theme.

Close your eyes and identify how you know you have an issue with unworthiness. In other words, where do you feel the unworthy feeling in your body?

Carry out the set-up phrase as normal: 'Even though I feel unworthy, I deeply and completely accept myself.'

Start to tap around the points with your eyes closed. Deeply tune into the feeling of unworthiness and occasionally repeat 'All this unworthiness' silently in your mind. Ask your subconscious to take you to the earliest memory that you have on this issue.

When a memory surfaces, carry out the EFT 'Tell the Story' technique, resolving all the aspects until it is a zero.

Now tune in to the same feeling again with your eyes closed and begin tapping around the points. This time, ask your subconscious to take you to the worst memory you have around unworthiness. Again, once a memory surfaces, carry out the 'Tell the Story' technique.

Finally, tune into the feeling again in the same way, still tapping, and ask your subconscious to bring to mind the most recent memory of unworthiness. Carry out the 'Tell the Story' technique on the memory.

Sometimes, collapsing the first, the worst and the most recent memory means that the whole pattern collapses. Other times you will find that you have to go in and resolve multiple memories. You may decide to resolve one a day, or if you are deeply committed to your healing, you could work on five or more a day. Ensure that you don't set your goals so high that it is unmanageable, or so low that it doesn't make an impact on your healing. You can either:

- Keep working through this exercise on its own until your VOC level on unworthiness is a zero.
- Or, continue working through the other exercises in this book simultaneously.

Whichever you do, prioritise healing your lack of unworthiness because it will deeply influence so many aspects of your healing journey, including your worthiness to actually heal.

## LACK OF SELF-LOVE

The second reason why you may be choosing not to live a full and satisfying life is a lack of self-love.

Self-love is a term that has been overused in the personal development industry. You may have read or heard that you should just 'love yourself'. However, if your programming gives you the opposite message, then you can find yourself in an internal conflict between thinking you *should* love yourself and actually feeling that love for yourself.

Before you can experience a profound sense of self-love, you need to be in a deep state of acceptance and forgiveness of yourself, which we will explore more in the third part of *The Healing Game* when we come to *Part C – The Transformer.*

Right now, as we are exploring the triggers, the key is to become more self-aware of that which may have contributed to a compromising of your dreams; a deep lack of self-love can be at the heart of your compromise.

Self-love is your natural state. We need to work with the conditions, programmes and experiences of your life that have taught you that you are unloveable. In other words, we are clearing the filters through which you are seeing yourself so that you can return to your natural state, rather than teaching you to love yourself.

## *David* – Multiple Sclerosis

David was brought up by his grandmother. His mother had disowned him and his father was unknown to him. He came to me with the belief, 'I'm not loveable' (even though he received lots of love from his grandmother). We used EFT to address all his childhood memories of feeling abandoned, unwanted and unloved. Although this did not cure his condition, it had a hugely positive effect on his symptoms and his self-perception.

---

### PROCESS FOR INCREASING SELF-LOVE

Take a VOC level on how much self-love you have right now, with 100 per cent being, 'I absolutely love myself,' and 10 per cent being, 'I barely love myself.'

We are going to look at this one quite deeply because often our conscious mind will tell us: 'Of course I love myself unconditionally.' However, the unconscious mind can be holding just the opposite

---

belief, which can be manifested as an unidentified or unnamed lack of self-love.

Close your eyes. Tune into your heart, and sit there for a few minutes. Be open to whatever it is you feel. You may be used to pushing away the feelings that are deep in your heart, but for this exercise, I invite you to get deeply in touch with them.

Now take the VOC level once again. Ask yourself how much self-love you have out of 100 per cent. If it isn't truly 100 per cent, then how do you know? Is it a feeling that you have? A thought in your mind that tells you: 'I'm just not loveable', or something else? Make a note in your journal.

Now, as we did for the unworthiness exercise, tap on the side of your hand and say out loud: 'Even though I don't fully love myself unconditionally, I accept myself as I am,' three times. Then start to tap around the points, still with your eyes closed, asking for the earliest memory to come up on this theme. As soon as you have located a memory, carry out the EFT 'Tell the Story' technique on the memory.

Now do the same again, asking for the worst memory to come up on this theme. As soon as you have located a memory, carry out the EFT 'Tell the Story' technique on the memory.

Then do the same, asking for the most recent memory to surface. As soon as you have located a memory, carry out the EFT 'Tell the Story' technique on the memory.

If this doesn't collapse the pattern, continue clearing between one and five memories a day, until your VOC level for self-love returns to 100 per cent.

With self-love, you might also need to start to become very vigilant about the way that you speak to yourself inside your mind. When we have lacked self-love, our self-talk often reflects this. I've seen the kindest and most loving people speaking to themselves in the harshest and most critical tone, and I've done the same to myself.

From here on in, I have a challenge for you. Picture a five-year-old child. One that has been emotionally battered, criticised and put down. If you had a chance to nurture such a child, I imagine that you would do so with the sweetest and gentlest of tones. That five-year-old child is you – or at least, your inner self, especially if you have become accustomed to speaking to yourself with anything other than the utmost love and respect. So as well as making a commitment to clear the life experiences that have contributed to a lack of self-love, you also need to meet yourself with love and kindness in every moment. It is going to take time, especially if it is a long-established pattern. But it is going to be one of the most radically transformational practices that you do.

## FEAR OF FAILURE (OR SUCCESS!)

Fear is the third contributing factor, which may have resulted in you holding back from your sense of purpose and compromising on your dreams. Whether it is fear of the judgement and criticism of others, or a holding back because of a fear of success, this fear is one of the things that might sit at the heart of any compromise of your satisfaction levels when you first got sick.

Just as you may have become accustomed to living with a lack of self-love, it is likely that, if you have been experiencing a low-level fear, it is something that you have assumed that you can't get beyond.

Fear is useful: it is a natural part of your wiring as a human being. It is useful when you are considering walking through a notoriously dubious neighbourhood: you feel it, and you decide to get a cab instead. It is less useful when you are considering living your life in a way that satisfies you and it crops up, meaning you pull back from your dreams.

If we look at why we get scared when we consider living our dreams, it is actually much simpler to understand with the model we are presenting in this book.

Early in your life you tried to do something and it didn't go well. And perhaps the adults around you didn't know how to help you effectively process what occurred. Maybe you were either criticised or humiliated for failing, or made to feel bad about your results. Your subconscious stored this information for future reference. Remember, it isn't working against you. It wants to keep you safe. That's its job. So, the next time you considered getting out of your comfort zone or stepping up, it reminded you of that feeling. That pattern is what has kept you small.

## *Brenda* – CHRONIC FATIGUE SYNDROME

Brenda was an artist who was afraid of promoting her work. In our first session, we worked on a specific memory, when she was nine years old. She had been about to give a presentation in class, and she dropped her notes on the floor. She couldn't get the pages in order and was told by the teacher that she was 'stupid'. This was a great humiliation for her, especially with the whole class watching, and she had retreated back into herself. We cleared the charge from this memory, and this had a profound effect on her symptoms. She had more energy, and less joint pain, and was able to put herself out in the world more, displaying at a local art exhibition.

With EFT, you can resolve your fear of failure or success on two levels. First and foremost, EFT is very good at dealing with the symptom of fear. This is because fear is a heightened emotion and it is great to use EFT to help you cope in the moment.

> **A quick reminder of how you would use EFT on a symptom such as fear:**
>
> 'Even though I have this _____ (feeling) in my _____ (location), I deeply and completely accept myself.'
>
> 'Even though I have this fear in my stomach, I deeply and completely accept myself.'

However, the real purpose of this book is not just to manage triggers, but to deal with the underlying causative factors.

This time we are looking for all the life experiences that have held you back. All the ones that have taught you to play small. All the ones that have squashed your dreams.

Some of these might simply be things that people have told you over and over again. For example, if your father or mother handed down to you a belief that 'Successful people are always corrupt,' then you might simply need to tap on this belief and take out any of the charge it has for you.

For example: 'Even though my mother/father told me that successful people are always corrupt, and it gives me a heaviness in my chest, I deeply and completely accept myself.'

There may also be specific memories with more than one aspect (emotional peak) that you have to deal with too. For example, you fell whilst running one of the most important races of your life. There may be several aspects such as hurting yourself as you hit the ground, the humiliation as others laughed, something your parents said when you got home, and the decision you made on that day to never run again.

## EXERCISE

Go through all your perceived failures, even the small ones, in this way, clearing them with EFT and using the 'Tell the Story' technique where relevant (if a memory is specific and has several peaks).

Now that we have looked at how to approach symptoms and have begun to clear any blocks that you might have to your life satisfaction, it's time to address *Component 3*: how you were showing up in your life at the time when the illness occurred.

# CHAPTER SIX

# Component 3
# SHOWING UP

IN THE THIRD COMPONENT of *The Healing Game*, we'll explore how you were showing up in the world when you became sick. This chapter is very personal and is going to require you to look within pretty deeply. You may need to look past some of the assumptions that you have made previously about the type of person that you are and the way you express yourself in the world.

How much of our personality is composed of responses, conditioned from how we have adapted to our environment, and how much is forged from the soul that we came into this world with, is not simple to determine. But there is one thing that I am quite sure about since I began the work that I do with EFT – our beliefs determine the way that we show up in the world, and those beliefs are determined by our life experiences.

There are a number of conditioned behavioural responses that can have an impact on your physiology. We've touched on a few of these before. For example, if you were showing up as what is termed a Type A personality who was highly motivated but was running the belief that you weren't accomplishing all that you could, you may have felt like you were constantly burning out. This could have been a major contributing factor to the breakdown of your body. Similarly, if you were a people pleaser who was consistently putting others first and never saying no, you could have burned yourself out in a different way.

## I JUST WANT THINGS TO BE
## THE WAY THEY WERE . . .

I have heard the following statement from so many of my clients when we start working together: 'I just want things to go back to the way they were before I was ill!'

Have you ever found yourself saying the same thing? Yet when I invite my clients to look closely at how their lives were before they got sick, it is often the last thing they actually want.

For many clients, the illness was an escape from a hectic, stressful and overwhelming life. This was certainly the case for me. I'm going to invite you, at this stage, to go deep within and ask yourself if it was the same for you. Because, however much you tell yourself that you want your 'old life' back (exactly as it was when you got sick), chances are there was something misaligned with the way you were showing up for your life before you actually got sick.

## *Richard* – ULCERATIVE COLITIS

Richard was a CEO of a computer software company. He burned the candle at both ends. He barely slept and worked long hours most days of the week. Eventually he was diagnosed with ulcerative colitis. He was no longer able to work his long hours, he had to completely change his diet and lifestyle, and he was always tired. We had to help him let go of his anger.  He was angry about being sick, and also about the amount of money he had spent so far on his healing.

## *Heather* – CHRONIC FATIGUE SYNDROME

In contrast, Heather was a stay-at-home mum. She attended all of her son's school events, cooked family meals (for the extended family too), hosted all the big celebrations, and couldn't say no when she was asked to commit to anything related to the family. Actually, she just wanted to be at home with her husband and son. She became overwhelmed and frustrated. She was diagnosed with chronic fatigue syndrome and was bed-bound a lot of the time.

First and foremost, if you have been doing the exercises from the previous chapter, and have begun to clear your blocks to unworthiness, self-love and fear of failure or success, then this chapter will be a bit easier to work through. The work we did in the last chapter will have paved the way for you to honestly examine how you were in the world when you got sick.

It would be so easy to slip into blame at this stage, which is why we want to support you to get into a practice of more self-love before you look at how you were showing up in the world. Just to clarify, and I can't reiterate this point enough, this chapter is not designed to give you fuel to blame yourself for your illness. Instead, it is designed to help you take responsibility for the kinds of habits and behaviours that you have developed, been taught, or conditioned into, that are not serving your health or sense of well-being, and to transform them accordingly. It is your chance to discover how your personality traits and behaviours are largely conditioned, and even though they feel as though they are you, many of them are actually not. We already began to change things at the core in the previous chapter, and this is going to help you do so even more deeply.

My traits were that I worked long hours as a teacher, had a three-hour commute every day, believed that having an afternoon nap was 'lazy' and a waste of precious time, and I was constantly looking to the next thing I should be accomplishing, even before I had finished the current thing I was focusing on.

In today's society, when someone explains that they are a Type A personality and an overachiever, it is often an acceptable explanation of why someone would drive themselves into the ground. However, the reality is that there is always a reason why someone shows up in life a certain way. That reason is usually driven by an underlying core belief.

My belief was, 'I will never amount to anything,' and this was something I was told by a teacher. Throughout my education, and when I started working, I did everything I could to prove to the world that I *could* amount to something, no matter how much time and energy it took. I was constantly trying to prove that teacher wrong.

We already started to address beliefs in the previous chapter when we looked at self-love and worthiness. Here, we can go even deeper.

Here's how it worked for me, and something that I see time and time again in clients. We think that the innate drive we have to keep going and to push ourselves is just 'who we are'. However, beyond this assumption, there is often a belief (either spoken or unspoken) that drives this. For example, maybe you have an unspoken sense that, to be loved, you have to be perfect, or that something or someone must change for you to be OK.

Beliefs such as these lead us to seek external validation from others in order to feel good about ourselves. The challenge here is that however much others validate you, it never feels like enough. This is because the belief is still the factor that is driving you, and the feeling around it very rarely changes. Sometimes, when you get approval, there is temporary relief. But when something else happens to retrigger it, you are back to feeling it again. What we are doing with this work is addressing and transforming the underlying cause.

## EXERCISE

Make a list of all the behaviours that were common to you at the time you got ill. Particularly include those that were part of the incessant drive for external validation from others. Here is a list of what I was doing:

- Working long hours without proper breaks
- Travelling a long distance to work on public transport
- Drinking most evenings
- Not exercising
- Constantly believing I could be doing more
- Being highly self-critical and unforgiving
- Putting everyone else before myself
- Couldn't say 'No'
- Didn't take time out for me and had no hobbies

Make your own list. I want to know everything, so we are going to take an inventory of all the elements of your life. Journal the following on how you were showing up:

- · With friends
- · In romantic relationships
- · At work
- · With family
- · Other social settings
- · With people that you didn't know very well
- · With yourself

For each one, what was the driving factor? Can you identify the belief associated with each behaviour? Were there any underlying fears, programmes or conditioned ways of being that felt like they were pushing you to be a certain way?

## Joyce

When she was a teenager, Joyce was told, 'You don't have a personality'. This led to her feeling invisible. No one was there for her, she felt invalidated and as though something was wrong with her.

She hadn't used her voice or spoken up to express her needs in her first marriage, or with her family, yet on the flip side had had a very high-powered job in a male dominant industry.

Now, remember, every limiting belief that you have is formed out of a decision you made about life when you were either told something over and over again, or when you experienced something traumatic that led you to make a conclusion about life.

Start breaking your beliefs down, one at a time. Ask yourself for each one – Who does this belong to? Is it actually mine? Where did I learn it? Did someone specifically teach me it? Remember, to play *The Healing Game* you are like a detective, searching for and uncovering each piece of the puzzle.

Carry out as much of the following as is applicable:

**Part One**

Tap on any phrases or beliefs that were handed down to you by relatives, significant adults and peers about who or how you should be in the world. For example, 'Even though my dad told me I'd have to work hard to be successful, I deeply and completely accept myself.'

If there is a relative or someone who has conditioned a certain response in you, we hope to get you beyond blaming them for this. To do this, you can add an additional part to the set-up statement if it helps or resonates. This additional part of the set-up statement involves forgiveness. It is not something that can be rushed. Forgiveness starts from within: in other words, with forgiving yourself. If it is something that creates a lot of triggers for you, it may be an issue that you want to tackle with a practitioner.

'Even though my dad told me that I have to push to achieve, and it gives me this sinking feeling in my chest, I deeply and completely accept myself, *and I'm working towards forgiving him for all that he taught me.*'

## Part Two

Use the 'Tell the Story' technique to resolve any specific memories that you have where you were conditioned to be a certain way in life. Of particular relevance are incidents where you were taught that it wasn't OK to be you, or that you had to be a certain way to fit in.

Go back to the run-up to your illness. Are there any specific memories or ways of being in the world that you didn't clear in the previous chapter? For example, did you have a boss that was pushing you really hard? If so, you can tap on the memories of things that they did or said. Remember to include all the senses (what you saw, heard and felt, but also anything you smelt or tasted).

You can also start to see how one set-up phrase might lead to another, or may trigger a related memory.

For example:

> 'Even though when my boss looked at me that way, I felt all this anxiety in my heart, I deeply and completely accept myself.'

This could lead to the underlying reason why you were triggered by your boss:

> 'Even though I felt all that anxiety in my heart because people must think well of me, I deeply and completely accept myself.'

This could then lead to an earlier memory that created the underlying belief that pins it altogether:

> 'Even though when my dad shouted at me that day, and I learnt I had to be perfect to be loved, I deeply accept myself now.'

**Part Three**

Make sure that you are also tapping on your reaction to your memories. These can include fear of losing your job, fear of what people might think if you didn't work super hard, deciding not to take the day off even when you were sick because you didn't want to let people down, and so on.

Now that we have begun to rewrite the trigger component, you probably have a better understanding of what was going on in your life on the run-up to the illness and how it impacted your health. If you have been carrying out the exercises in this book, then some kind of transformation is hopefully taking place.

In the next section, we are going to explore THE CONNECTOR. This section will deepen your connection to your true, authentic self. We will be helping you to define exactly who you are beyond your conditioning and programming, asking why you can't live from that place all the time, and then beginning to explore what would happen if you did. All three parts of THE CONNECTOR contain transformational tools to help you connect deeply to who you truly are.

# THE CONNECTOR

# CHAPTER SEVEN

# Component 4
# THE GATEWAY

IN THIS CHAPTER, we are going to explore a question that might, at first glance, seem like a philosophical one. I am going to be asking you: 'Who are you, beyond your triggers, beliefs and programmes?'

Truthfully, asking this question within *The Healing Game* is actually far from philosophical. In fact, if there was one question that summarised the essence of what we are doing together, one question that sat at the heart of all the tapping, and the clearing, and the transformation that is taking place as you work through this book, it would be this one.

'Who you are' is *not* your emotions, or your triggers, or your programmes, or your beliefs, or your patterns or any of your other behaviours. It is simply that you have been taught to identify with these things, as if they were actually you. You have been trained to attach your-self to your beliefs and to fight for them. You have been conditioned to be triggered by your experiences and react to your emotions, to the point where, even if it causes you discomfort or pain, you might find yourself vehemently defending your point of view.

## IT'S NOT ABOUT HAVING NO EMOTIONS, EITHER

Some spiritual or growth paths teach dispassion. A number of these paths teach their students to be void of emotions, as though emotions were actually the source of the problem. Students learn how to be free of their emotional experiences by not having any emotional reactions, or at least by aiming to not have any.

### Samantha – LUPUS

Samantha didn't want anyone to see her vulnerable side. She was afraid if she started crying that she'd fall apart and not be able to pull herself together again. She refused to allow herself to cry during her first marriage.

During our EFT sessions, she went from feeling embar-rassed when she cried, to accepting that it was OK to cry, and then she cried freely.

### *Betty* – PERITONITIS AND CHRONIC FATIGUE

Betty was afraid to laugh and have fun. She believed 'something was wrong with her' and people wouldn't want to be around her if they really knew her.

We used EFT to address the times she'd shut down because she was told she was 'over the top'. Once she had permission to let go, she laughed and snorted in our sessions. She was soon able to laugh in everyday situations again too.

You are a human being with a human nervous system. You do not have to transcend that fact in order to experience peace. What you are learning to do in the course of this book is to exist alongside your emotional system. To fully feel every emotion that you experience but to no longer be governed by your emotions.

During the graduation ceremony for Advanced EFT Practitioners I held in August 2014, I welled up with emotion when I gave one student her certificate. I was so proud of her for overcoming all her limiting beliefs and fears, that I burst into tears, and cried in front of a room full of students. When I stopped and looked up, every student was crying with me! It is natural for us to release emotion in this way and to share a common experience.

What I want to invite you to understand is the difference between your emotional reaction to something, which has been created by your life experiences, and the truth of who you really are beneath your patterns and programmes.

In this book we are helping you to begin to unravel all this. You have been so used to a thought becoming a feeling and then attaching to that feeling as though it is a reality. Here, we are supporting you to have a different experience. EFT can help you do just that.

**EXERCISE**

**The Difference Between a Thought and a Feeling**

Think of a thought that triggers you. We'll use one that is common for most people that I work with who are overcoming long-term illness:

'I'll never recover.'

See if this thought has a charge for you. If it doesn't, choose a thought that does have a charge for you.

Notice that when you think the thought, how it quickly becomes a feeling. In other words, where do you feel the charge of the thought in your body? What is the emotion attached to it?

Now carry out the EFT tapping exercise on the thought:

'Even though I'm afraid I'll never recover, and this thought gives me a _____ (feeling) in my _____ (location), I deeply and completely accept myself.'

Carry out several rounds of tapping until the feeling attached to the thought starts to subside.

Now, here is the interesting thing. Assuming you have taken the charge out of that thought, does it still have the same impact? Do you believe it as much? The likelihood is that your *perception* about the thought changed when you did not feel so strongly about it.

Fully grasping this exercise could be one of the most evolutionary things you do for yourself on your healing journey. If you are able to transform the weight of any thought that you have, then your thoughts and their accompanying feelings no longer have power over you. You can release identification with any thought. Your thoughts and accompanying feelings cease to become your identity.

Many spiritual paths talk about awakening. It is often seen as some kind of glorified or heightened experience. In truth, it is just you remembering who you are beyond your patterns and programmes – it is just you remembering your true essence. One spiritual teacher, Adyashanti, calls it 'a change of occupancy.' Your conditioned or programmed self is no longer centre stage and running the show. You are aware of all your conditioning and your programming, but it is not what rules you anymore. Your conscious awareness is centre stage instead.

## AWARENESS

One of the main things we are doing here is increasing your awareness. This is a two-pronged approach. First and foremost, we want to help you to experience your life beyond your triggers and programmes so that you are operating from awareness. Also, we want to help you to increase your awareness of when your triggers and patterns show up, so that you can transform them.

The EFT tapping exercises in this book have been helping you to increase your awareness in general. Up until the point that we started working together, you may have experienced your buttons being pushed, and had the sense that you had no power to do anything about that. As we started working together, hopefully you began to experience more self-awareness and a higher level of self-management of your emotions. The next step is to become instantly aware if you do get triggered, so you can resolve the trigger with EFT.

First of all, it helps to have a plan of what you are going to do when you are triggered, and to create that plan when you are not triggered.

## EXERCISE
### How Do I Know When I am Triggered?

Think back to the last time you were triggered. What changes took place in your physical body? What kind of thoughts did you have that you attached to? What kind of feelings did it create for you? What were your reactions as a result? Did you have a feeling that you were being taken over and that your body wasn't yours?

Journal the common things you experience, say or do when you are triggered.

The next time you are triggered, the idea is to transform your trigger as soon as possible using the EFT Tapping Protocol. The *second* you notice you have been triggered, pause, and begin tapping. If you are very triggered, you might not even be able to think of a set-up statement. You may just have to start tapping. You could even pick one of the tapping points – an emergency point – that you can begin tapping on, if you can't think of anything else to do.

### *Emma* – Lupus, Anaemia

Every time Emma felt like a failure during her illness, she tapped on:
- the feeling
- the trigger (what had just happened to make her feel that way)
- how her body felt
- what she was thinking
- how she reacted to the situation.

This prevented her from slipping down into her thoughts and feelings of somehow having failed because she was ill.

It will probably take you a few attempts before you are able to do this straight away. It can help, if you picture it like a book. For the first few times that you get triggered, you might find you are on Chapter 5 before you realise. You tap, you release the feeling, you have some awareness and you experience a perceptual shift. Then next time, you get to the end of the first chapter before you realise you are triggered. Again you go through the process. Eventually, you find yourself waking up when you get to the end of the first page. With practice, with increased awareness, and using the EFT Tapping Protocol, you will find yourself simultaneously getting triggered and becoming conscious at the same time. When you add to this the fact that the more you clear your underlying memories, patterns and programmes using the EFT 'Tell the Story' technique, the less likely you are to get triggered, you'll find that you'll experience life much more through conscious awareness than through the filters of your conditioned mind.

## MEDITATION

There are, of course, other things you can do to experience more of your life through conscious awareness and less through the perception of your conditioned self. Meditation and Mindfulness are two such practices, and, although it is beyond the scope of this book to teach you to effectively meditate, I recommend practices that enable you to sit in stillness and observe the patterns of the conditioned mind. Two resources worth checking out are the books *Mind Calm* and *Thunk!* by Sandy C. Newbigging (see *Bibliography* for more details).

## EXERCISE

This is something that I used to do when I was ill, to stop my mind racing when I needed to sleep in the afternoon:

Focus on the soles of your feet. Breathe into that area, and as you breathe out, say in your mind, 'I release.' Then focus on your ankles, and breathe into that area, and as you breathe out, say in your mind, 'I release.'
Then focus on your calves, and breathe into that area, and as you breathe out, say in your mind, 'I release.'
Continue working your way up the body in the same way, until you reach the top of your head.

Now that we have begun to explore who you are beyond your conditioning, programming, patterns and behaviours, in the next chapter we are going to explore more deeply why, so far, you haven't been able to live from beyond your conditioning.

# CHAPTER EIGHT

# Component 5
# WHY CAN'T I . . . ?

I N THE LAST CHAPTER we began to look at *The Gateway* to your true, authentic self. We started to explore who you are beyond your conditioning and your life experiences. In this chapter we are going to explore any remaining pro-grammes that are preventing you from showing up in your life *as* your true, authentic self.

If you haven't worked with a practitioner so far, you might want to consider doing so to support your work in this section. I suggest this, because we can't always see our own blind spots. Some of our beliefs, behaviours and ways of showing up in the world have become so engrained through repetition and reinforcement, that we aren't actually aware that there is a reality beyond them. We mistakenly believe that they are who we truly are.

So, in this chapter, we are going to begin playing with the question: 'Why can't I show up in the world as my true, authentic self?' Your answers to this question will provide vital clues as to how your perceptions and beliefs have been limiting you and holding you back.

## UNCOVERING YOUR CORE BELIEFS

Your core beliefs form the glue that has so far held your life together. In *Transform Your Beliefs, Transform Your Life: EFT Tapping Using Matrix Reimprinting*, Karl Dawson and Kate Marrilat highlight how crucial it is to uncover and transform your core beliefs if you want to initiate true healing.

Matrix Reimprinting has its main focus on the role that beliefs play in our health and well-being.

Remember in *Symptoms*, Chapter 4, we started to explore what was happening in your life when you became ill? We began to look for specific events that may have contributed to your condition, as well as things that may have occurred in the first six years of your life that compromised your sense of safety. What we were actually looking for was an event (or a number of events) that occurred in your life that created a limiting belief. Because, when you experienced a stress or trauma and you were not able to cope with it biologically, your physiology adapted to be able to cope. In that moment, a belief was formed. Some examples of beliefs that could have formed in that moment include:

- The world is a dangerous place
- It is not safe to be me
- I have to be perfect to be loved
- Something must change for me to be OK
- People can't be trusted
- People are out to get me
- The world is against me
- All men are _____
- All women are _____
- I'm not good/smart/fast/fit/thin/strong/independent enough
- I'm too fat/thin/old/young/sensitive/tough
- Good things don't last
- The other shoe is about to drop
- I'm not seen/heard/listened to

And so on.

In your journal, answer the following:

1. Who told you that you were 'too _____' or 'not _____ enough'? Why?
2. What impact did these messages have on you? For example, I always played small, or I put my needs last.
3. What mask have you worn as a result of this? For example, I became a workaholic, or I became sick.

4. When did you learn that it was not OK to be you?
5. What would happen if you were truly authentic/ really yourself in all situations?
6. What would happen if you were vulnerable in all situations?

Again, the reason that you formed these beliefs is that your subconscious mind was trying to keep you safe. It was attempting to make a conclusion about the world so that you didn't make the same mistake again. These conclusions have likely become the blueprint by which you live. And if that is the case, while they served you once, it is also likely that they are not serving you now.

**EXERCISE**

Again, I ask you: 'Why can't you show up as your true, authentic self?' In your journal, answer this question. Let your answers flow freely from you. Give all the reasons why this is true for you. Your list might start with a conclusion-based statement such as:

· It's not possible for me to . . .
· I can't . . .
· I have to . . .
· I'm afraid to . . .
· I should . . .

· I shouldn't . . .

· If I did X, then Y would happen

And so on.

You might find yourself saying things along the lines of:
· If I speak my truth, X won't love me anymore
· I have to stay in this relationship because X supported me while I was ill and I owe it to him/her
· When I recover, I have to return to my old job because it's the only thing I know how to do
· I'm afraid to set boundaries because I don't want to hurt people

What we are addressing here, at the core, is the unfulfilling roles that you have been playing. This work is about recognising where you have been in the role of you, then removing your mask, and living authentically.

### Sheila – ADRENAL FATIGUE, MULTIPLE CHEMICAL SENSITIVITIES

Sheila had an unpredictable upbringing. She always felt different from her siblings and didn't feel loved by her parents. She grew up with the belief that 'the world is a dangerous place'.

Sheila's husband offered stability, safety, money, security, and supported her whilst she was ill. She felt that she owed it to him to stay in the relationship, although on other levels she was totally unfulfilled.

Through EFT we addressed how she could fulfil herself through developing the things she loved. Her confidence began to grow; she started socialising, and found a new depth to her own life. We resolved the belief that the world is a dangerous place, and she was able to flourish accordingly.

If you are someone that has lived without boundaries and been a people pleaser, then this is going to push so many buttons for you. But we have to address this element because otherwise you are going to go back to those unfulfilling roles that you played before you got sick. And the very thought of doing so may be keeping you locked in a pattern of sickness.

## *Richard* – Fibromyalgia

Although married with children, Richard lived by his parents' rules. At family gatherings, he wanted to speak up but was afraid of conflict, of what others would think and of losing his family's love. Richard always believed that his parents preferred his sister.

Incrementally, we addressed each time he had felt unheard, dismissed or criticised. He started to gain confidence and self-respect. Eventually he was able to speak up, and even started to turn down some family gatherings when he chose to.

Assuming that there is a sense that you don't want to go back to being the stay-at-home mum with three kids who never has time to herself, or the guy that goes to the office and stays there fourteen hours a day, or whatever other role you have been playing, then this next section is going to help you get beyond operating from your belief systems.

## PROTOCOL FOR CLEARING BELIEFS

Here is a variation on an earlier exercise taken from *Matrix Reimprinting Using EFT*.

Working on one belief at a time, give the belief a VOC score (Validity of Cognition), with 100 per cent being you totally believe it, and 10 per cent being it is barely true for you.

### Slow Tap

Now tap on the side of your hand, using your belief as a set-up statement. For example, 'Even though I have to be perfect to be loved, I deeply and completely accept myself.'

With your eyes closed start tapping on one point

slowly and gently. At the same time repeat the belief silently in your mind: 'I have to be perfect to be loved.' Then pause for a few moments. Repeat it once again, still silently in your mind. Stay on the same point for a longer time than usual, before moving to the next point. Ensure the pressure is soft when you tap. The reason we tap slowly and gently, repeating the belief silently with our eyes closed is that it takes us into a more hypnotic state and allows a memory to surface.

Each time you repeat the belief, be open to a memory surfacing. As soon as a memory surfaces, use the 'Tell the Story' technique to resolve it.

You can then begin the whole process again, using the same belief as a set-up phrase as you tap on the side of your hand, then tapping slowly around the points in turn, repeating the reminder phrase until a memory surfaces. Each time you find a new memory, use the 'Tell the Story' technique to resolve it.

Keep repeating this procedure until the VOC level is a zero for that particular belief. You might not get the VOC level to a zero in one sitting of tapping: it might take several sittings, particularly if the belief is supported by a lot of memories on the same theme.

Once you have got your VOC level to a zero, in a future sitting you can work on another belief.

Referring back to Matrix Reimprinting, there is a vital aspect of this work that you are doing here that cannot be overlooked when it comes to rewriting beliefs. And that is, 'What did you learn about life on that day and what do you need to know, so that you can feel like you are safe and that the danger has passed?'

Even though it is beyond the scope of this book to teach you the full, advanced emotional freedom technique, Matrix Reimprinting, if you can get into the habit of asking this question when you do your belief work, it will heighten the results you get. If you learnt that the world was a dangerous place, for example, ensure you include a round of EFT on:

'Even though I learnt that the world is a dangerous place, I deeply and completely accept myself.'

When you have taken the charge out of this statement, you can check in with yourself about what belief you need to install in place of the old one, and replace it in the following way:

'Even though I learnt _____ (old belief), I deeply and completely accept myself, and am now choosing to believe _____ (new belief).'

Example: 'Even though I learnt that the world is a dangerous place, I deeply and completely accept myself, and am now choosing to believe that I am safe and all is well.'

You can then alternate your reminder phrases by tapping the old belief and the new one, always ending on the new one.

For example:

**Top of the head:** The world is a dangerous place.
**Eyebrow:** I'm safe and all is well.
**Side of the eye:** The world is a dangerous place.
**Under the eye:** I'm safe and all is well.

And so on.

Do this until the old belief no longer has any charge and the new belief feels like it is true for you, at least in the particular memory you are working on. You will know that it is true for you when you have a perceptual shift: I *am* safe, it is over, I survived.

## EVOLVING THE PERSONAL PEACE PROCEDURE

In conventional EFT, there is a process called 'The Personal Peace Procedure' in which you write down every single negative or impactful life experience you had and work through them, one a day, for 365 days. Although I have a great respect for this process, it can leave you feeling overwhelmed, and it can also take some time to get to the memories that are causing you challenges in your current life. I prefer working through the core beliefs one by one, because it means that you actually impact and resolve the memories that have created negative core beliefs. We get to the issue right at the root, and create lasting change where it is most beneficial.

Now that we have explored why, up until now, you haven't been able to show up in your life the way that you may have liked to, in the next chapter we are going to begin to envision your life the way you would like it to be when you aren't being run by your core beliefs.

# CHAPTER NINE

# Component 6
# WHAT WOULD
# HAPPEN IF . . . ?

A T THIS POINT, you have hopefully cleared a significant number of your core beliefs, which have probably been holding you in a pattern of behaviours based on your filters. Following this, it is time to address what your life is actually going to be like, now that you are not operating predominantly through a preconceived idea of who you should be. In this chapter we are going to ask the question:

'What would your life be like if you showed up as your true, authentic self all of the time?'

This chapter is about your vision. It is about your vision for your life, your relationships, your career, your health, your wealth, your spiritual path, your creativity and everything else that lights you on fire.

If there is any doubt that you fully deserve to live the life of your wildest dreams, then there is still more clearing to do with reference to the chapter that preceded this one. If you have done all that you can by yourself, you might want to consider a practitioner to help you to clear any blocks that you have to living to your fullest potential.

Assuming your foot is off the brake and you are fully aligned with transforming your world, the following will help you create a vision of what you are looking for. We will create your vision here, and then, in *Taking Action*, Chapter 12, we will help you fully implement it.

## EXERCISE

If you are visual, you might want to spend some time creating a vision board, a mind map, or even a mind movie of how you envisage your life. You could include pictures, photographs, images and so on. And, when you choose your images and pictures, ensure that they do not include pictures of you that have associations with how your life was before you became sick, or how it has been since then.

Here is the key. When you start working through the following and triggers come up around deserving to live a full life in some or all of the following areas, you can resolve them with EFT. The aim is to create a life without limits.

You may want to complete the following, one day at a time, so you can carefully consider each aspect that is being presented, and begin to connect with the associated activities without overwhelming yourself.

## WORKING LIFE

What is your life purpose? Putting aside everything you have trained in and qualified in so far, what do you really want to do? What would you do if there were no perceived limits? What did you love to do as a child, that may have been pushed aside by your parents or by a preconceived idea of who you should be?

You may need to spend days, weeks or longer getting in touch with your purpose and finding out what you are here for. This is usually a process, rather than something that comes to you instantly, particularly if you have blocked this off for some time.

**EXERCISE**

When you have identified your purpose, what could you do to take steps towards your purpose today? Take one step in the direction of your new or reawakened purpose. The idea is to have the 'box ticked', so that, even if there are a host of things that you need to do before a career change, you do something small, and frequently, to begin to design your new working life.

## FAMILY AND RELATIONSHIPS

What do your ideal relationships look like? What would you like to create more of in terms of relationships and connections? What kinds of people would you like to spend more time with?

**EXERCISE**

Reach out to one person that you have lost touch with since you were sick. Ensure that you focus on reconnecting as well as sharing your healing journey with them.

## ENVIRONMENT

What would you like your house to look like? Take an inventory of each room. What can you get rid of to create more space? What would you like to add? In the longer term, would you like to move altogether? Where would you like to live?

## EXERCISE

Do one thing that changes your relationship with your personal environment. Call up a charity to come and take something away that no longer resonates with you. Recycle something.

## CREATIVITY

What creative activities fill you with joy? What makes your heart sing? What did you enjoy as a child that you may have lost touch with as an adult?

## EXERCISE

What can you do today to experience more creativity in your life? Take one action towards developing a hobby, starting a new creative activity, or return to something you did as a child that you dropped.

## JOY AND FUN

What kinds of things do you like doing for fun? Is there anything that you haven't tried before, that you would really like to try? Are there places you would like to travel to that you haven't travelled to yet? Are there things from childhood that you lost touch with that you could rekindle? We are primarily looking for activities that increase your endorphins and/or your sense of connection.

## EXERCISE

Do one thing today that brings you joy and fun.

Now that we have designed your ideal life, and begun to play with some small changes in the real world, the next section, THE TRANSFORMER, is going to help you to fully implement those changes.

We'll address any fear that you may have about recovering, help you surrender to your current circumstances so you can heal from that place (which is very different to giving in to your condition, as we highlighted previously), and also look at what you need to do to put the life that you have envisaged in this chapter into action.

# THE TRANSFORMER

# CHAPTER TEN

# Component 7
# ADDRESSING THE FEAR

COMPONENT 7 is about addressing any fear that you may have to implementing the changes that we've highlighted in the course of this book.

Your fear around healing is like the elephant in the room that nobody wants to talk about. First of all, it probably doesn't make any sense on a conscious level if you have an underlying fear to heal, because we are hard-wired for survival. But when we look at your fears around healing, we are actually addressing what it means to show up and live your life fully and freely. So, this chapter is really about addressing any fears that you have around healing so that you can fully transform.

## FEAR OF LOSING SUPPORT

The first fear that we want to address is moving out of the support system that may have been created by you and for you. If you have had a carer or a partner supporting you whilst you healed, you may have found that you slipped into codependent patterns.

It's not just the person who has been sick who needs to consider whether they have fallen into codependent patterns. They also occur for the carer themselves, particularly if they have formed an identity around caring and it has given them a sense of purpose in the world.

There is also the fear of loss if you have been experiencing intensive care from someone. It is a basic human response. Deep down inside, and especially if we did not receive the comfort and support that we would have liked as a child, we all have a basic need to be held. Being cared for in long-term illness fulfils this need, and we can find ourselves triggered into a primal response of not wanting to let that go.

**EXERCISE**

Check in with yourself to see if you have any of this fear, and if you do, use the EFT Tapping Protocol to release it:

'Even though I am fearful of stepping out alone, I deeply and completely accept myself.'

'Even though there is a part of me that doesn't want

to let go of being cared for in this way, I deeply and completely accept myself.'

## FEAR OF LOSING FINANCIAL BENEFITS

Another thing that I have seen frequently is the pattern of keeping ourselves sick so that we don't lose benefits. This can sound like quite a harsh one, but in reality, if you have been receiving financial cushioning from benefits, it can be hard to let go of it. This is because we can be triggered into survival by the fear of losing our financial support.

If this is the case, you can use the EFT Tapping Protocol to resolve it:

'Even though I have all this terror in my heart at the thought of losing my benefits, I deeply and completely accept myself.'

'Even though I am triggered into survival and I have this churning in my stomach at the thought of losing my benefits, I deeply and completely accept myself.'

This doesn't apply just to benefits, but also to any other financial support you may stand to lose when you are back on your own two feet again. If this is intertwined with a codependent relationship, it can mean that there are layers of challenges that are affecting you. Again, you may need a practitioner to help you uncover these if they are deeply rooted.

## FEAR OF SLIPPING BACK INTO
## OLD PATTERNS AND ROLES

Another fear is of slipping back into old patterns or roles that are no longer serving you. It is all very well to make a vow that you are going to change, when you are sick. The illness becomes a very strong motivator. Often we make a conscious vow to transform when such a motivator is in place. But at the same time, we don't always trust ourselves to do the right thing. Examples include returning to putting others' needs before your own, overworking, or skipping yoga practice or meditation.

## SUBCONSCIOUS VOWS AND CONFLICTS

The reason we often find ourselves with one foot on the brake and the other on the accelerator is that we have a subconscious vow that conflicts with our conscious vow to get well. If we have conflicting vows, they are known as subconscious conflicts. These are the ones that make us feel like we are going forward and going backwards at the same time. For example, 'I really am going to heal (conscious vow), *but deep down I'm afraid that if I do, I will have to go back to my old job*' (subconscious conflict).

## EXERCISE

Check yourself for any conscious or unconscious vows, or conflicts, that you might have about slipping back into old roles or old ways. You are mainly searching for a deep, underlying lack of trust that you might have in yourself that you can truly create changes. If you locate such a feeling, carry out the EFT Tapping Protocol:

'Even though I fear that I cannot change _____ (habit or behaviour), I deeply and completely accept myself.'

'Even though I worry that I will fall back into my old role of _____, I deeply and completely accept myself.'

## WHAT DO YOU GET OUT OF BEING ILL?

It can be quite a confronting question, but in reality there are often hidden payoffs to illness. You get time to yourself, for a start. Also, you may have found that you actually deepened your connection to yourself when you were sick. Maybe you read and researched more, gained a deeper understanding of the human condition, and so on. Perhaps you are far more conscious than you ever were previously. Illness may have given you more time to learn yoga, to meditate, and to walk in nature. Perhaps you deepened your understanding of alternative medicine and therapies, and are beginning to enjoy the new perspective and life views you have, and these could conflict with your old world significantly.

## EXERCISE

First highlight any fears you have about losing what you have gained while you have been ill. Now formulate them into tapping statements.

For example:

'Even though I'm afraid that there will be no time for me when I am well, I deeply and completely accept myself.'

'Even though I'm concerned that I won't get to read or research when I am well again, I deeply and completely accept myself.'

'Even though I don't want to lose touch with my spiritual connection if I go back to work, I deeply and completely accept myself.'

## *Samantha* – Crohn's Disease

When Samantha got sick, she really found herself. At the same time, she started harbouring a fear of losing herself when she recovered. She was afraid of returning to the hamster wheel and losing the spiritual connection she had gained. She enjoyed researching her illness, cooking nourishing food, reading, meditating and respecting her body.

We used EFT to address her belief that none of this would be possible if she healed and started working again. We cleared all her stressors around work and how hard it was. We also addressed how to set boundaries with her father. She had been his carer for some time, and the illness offered her time out from that.

## ILLNESS AS A BOUNDARY SETTER

Another aspect to consider is that illness may have been your only means of setting boundaries. If you are someone who didn't learn to say no before you got sick, then being ill might have provided this opportunity for you. You have probably found that you absolutely had to learn to say no to some things, particularly if you were bed-bound. Illness can be our 'get out of jail free' card at times, and can mean that we use it as a reason for not doing something, when the real reason is that we don't actually want to do it. We often learn to hide behind the illness and it becomes a defence or wall that we use to avoid speaking our truth. There is no blame here. I have done this on numerous occasions in the past, myself. The antidote to this is to clear our fear of speaking our truth.

## EXERCISE

Without judgement, highlight anywhere you have been using illness as a 'get out of jail free' card, and use the EFT Tapping Protocol.

For example:

'Even though I've been hiding behind the illness and have been afraid to speak my truth to _____, I deeply and completely accept myself.'

'Even though I'm concerned that if I'm well, I won't have any excuse not to _____, I deeply and completely accept myself.'

## SELF-EXPECTATIONS

Another type of fear can come from the expectations you had placed on yourself. Often we have a high level of expectation for what we should achieve in life, but we let this relax a little when we are ill. Somewhere in your mind, there will probably be the thought, 'When I am better, I can make up for it,' or 'When I am recovered, I can get back on track with my life mission.' If you have been creating pressure around this, or, as I did, you've placed an unreasonable amount of expectations upon yourself, it can be challenging to think about returning to this way of life.

## EXERCISE

Identify all your expectations of, and projections upon, yourself and use the EFT Tapping Protocol to clear them. For example:

> 'Even though I've been putting pressure on myself to _____, I deeply and completely accept myself.'
> 'Even though when I'm well I'll expect myself to _____, I deeply and completely accept myself.'

### *Pam* – ULCERATIVE COLITIS, FIBROMYALGIA, MULTIPLE CHEMICAL SENSITIVITIES

Pam was a journalist in the city and a Type A personality. When she crashed physically, she returned to her family home to recover. She was desperate to get her old life back, but the payoff would be that she'd have to return to her old job.

We addressed her underlying driving factors with EFT. She had traumatic memories of her mother dying when she was a child. She'd had to grow up fast and become responsible and there was still some unresolved anger around being left by her mother. She began to understand that she'd pushed herself to avoid the pain of her childhood (something I've seen in many cases). Illness offered her time off from work, and time with her father, which she hadn't had as a child.

## EXPECTATIONS FROM OTHERS

As well as the expectations you place on yourself, what about the expectations from the other people in your life? This can include bosses, work colleagues, friends, family members and so on. You may have found that you played a role or wore a mask with certain people, and that the illness gave you a relief from that role. Maybe there is an underlying fear of returning to those roles when you get well again. Perhaps there is even a subtle social pressure for you to be functioning and contributing to society once more.

If you are a parent, you may have even found that the illness gave you some kind of break from your role as a full-time parent, as other family members rallied around to help you cope. A subtle fear of having to cope as you did prior to the illness can also act as a subconscious conflict.

Expectations from others can also be tied into the workings of a relationship that you know needs to end, but you have been staying with him/her because of the condition that you are currently in.

## EXERCISE

Identify any expectations from external sources that feel like an underlying pressure to you, and use the EFT Tapping Protocol to clear them.

For example:

'Even though there are expectations from _____ that make me feel _____, I deeply and completely accept myself.'

'Even though I will be required to be number one at _____ again when I return to health, I deeply and completely accept myself.'

'Even though I will be required to be a fully functional member of society, I deeply and completely accept myself.'

'Even though I have all this _____ (emotion) around being a full-time parent again, I deeply and completely accept myself.'

'Even though I know my current relationship is over, I deeply and completely accept myself.'

## WORK AND LIFE PURPOSE

How you actually feel about working, returning to work or even starting a new career can also be acting as an unconscious stressor. Having to return to a job you hate, or if you know that you can't go back, but still don't know what your life purpose is or what you are going to do next: all these are examples of unconscious conflicts.

### *Laurie* – Chronic Fatigue Syndrome, Depression

Laurie had been sick for over 10 years. She lived with her parents, had lost all her friends and wasn't able to work. The illness gave her a purpose and reason to not be out in the world. At the same time, she constantly compared herself to her sister.

Using EFT, we addressed all the times that Laurie had moved to different locations as a child. She'd been to various schools, had demanding parents, and been a high achiever. We addressed the pressure she felt from her parents, her lack of purpose and not knowing where she fitted in. Her self-confidence increased, she became more aware of her talents and she stopped comparing herself to her sister.

**EXERCISE**

Identify any work or career conflicts that you are experiencing and use the EFT Tapping Protocol to clear them. For example:

'Even though I hate my boss, I deeply and completely accept myself.'

'Even though I don't want to go back to my old job, I deeply and completely accept myself.'

'Even though I don't know my purpose, I deeply and completely accept myself.'

You have probably already got the sense that this component is essential and that it is also multi-dimensional. The key point to remember here is that fear is one of the major emotions that keeps us in stress and prevents the body from healing. Far from avoiding the fear, or feeling the fear and doing it anyway, hopefully during this chapter you have been able to face it head on. Some of the fears you may already have been aware of. Others might be new to you. I advise you to be as thorough as you can to clear the underlying fears (which are ultimately the feelings that give you the sense that you are sabotaging your success) before we move on to the next section.

Once you have addressed the underlying fears that you might have about healing, move on to the next chapter, where we are going to explore surrendering to your condition.

# CHAPTER ELEVEN

# Component 8
# SURRENDER

O UT OF ALL THE COMPONENTS of *The Healing Game*, the concept of surrender is probably the one that causes the most resistance. In fact, some clients have become downright angry when I have talked to them about surrender. I totally understand if the concept of surrendering pushes a button in you. For many of us, it is confused with giving in to your condition.

Throughout human evolution, right down to this present day, we have been largely programmed to fight that which we do not accept. Even though there is often a part of our consciousness that knows deep down inside that war is not the answer, we are at war on countless levels. There is a 'war on drugs' and a 'war on terrorism'. There is even a 'war on cancer'.

This fighting spirit is a socially acceptable part of our human nature. Yet fighting that which we do not want in life creates major resistance. You have probably heard the popular phrase in personal development that *what we resist persists*. From an attraction standpoint you are probably already aware that the more you focus on something that you don't want, the more you reinforce it. But we are going much deeper on that journey when we play *The Healing Game*. So, for this component of the game I want to first look at what resistance is doing to your physical body, and then work with you so you can experience a healthy level of surrender and counteract the challenges that resistance may be causing you.

## MORE ON RESISTANCE

Were you ever divided about something? Part of you wanted one thing and part of you wanted another. Think back to that division and how it felt to be split in that way. What happened in your body when you were? Being split takes up a lot of physical and emotional energy. It feels as though your soul is torn two ways and you are literally being pulled in half. As though there are two yous – one that wants one thing and one that wants another.

Before I was sick, I spent years knowing I was in a relationship that wasn't fulfilling me, yet I was torn on a daily basis between whether I should stay or leave.

### *Paula* – Lyme Disease

Not long after she was married, Paula's husband started drinking heavily. Always quite religious, Paula suddenly lost her connection to God.

Paula believed she couldn't trust her husband and simultaneously, that she was a 'burden' to him because of her illness. She wanted to leave but was worried about money and how she'd survive. We worked on her chest pains and racing heart when she thought about leaving, enabling her to make a decision from a place that was much less fear- and stress-based.

Now compare being torn apart to when you are fully aligned with something, totally committed to a single goal with clarity and purpose. All your boxes are ticked and you are fully lined up with that which you are doing.

Resistance carries a very similar energy to being divided. There is part of you that is experiencing reality as it currently is, and another part that is pushing it away or fighting it. The trouble is that it means you can very rarely be present when you are resisting what is. You either find yourself in a future moment, fantasizing about a time when you are healed, or you transport yourself back to the past, longing for how things were before. This push and pull not only drains your valuable emotional resources that would be better used for healing, but it also impacts on your contentment levels, your endorphin levels, and it can leave you feeling disconnected from the world around you for the majority of the time. It reinforces your attitude that healing equals struggle and, particularly if you are on a long-term healing journey, it can make the whole experience extremely unappealing.

## TAPPING ON RESISTANCE

As with all the EFT exercises in this book, it is not just the resistant thought that we want to address, but also the accompanying emotional feeling.

Out of 100 per cent, how resistant are you to your condition right now, with 100 being 'totally resistant' and 0 being 'not resistant at all'? Make a note.

---

### LEVEL 1 – THE RESISTANT THOUGHT

First of all, identify the resistant thoughts that are the biggest stressors for you. You may recognise them in the list below or you might have your own specific ones:

· I'll never heal
· I'm always going to be sick
· I wish things would go back to the way they were
· I'm not loveable unless I'm healed

---

· I'm no use to anyone in this state

· I'm a burden

Now, choose one and see if it has an accompanying feeling in your body. Where do you feel it and what is the intensity? For example:

· Anger in the chest

· Heaviness in the heart

· Sinking feeling in the stomach

Take a SUDs level (out of 10) to measure the intensity of the resistant thought and its accompanying physical feeling(s). Address this using EFT and when the SUDs level is zero, address the remaining resistant thoughts one by one, using EFT.

> For example: 'Even though I've got this anger in my chest at the thought that I'll never heal, I deeply and completely accept myself.'

Work through each resistant thought using EFT, until the charge has been taken out of each one. You can repeat this exercise any time that you start to experience resistance. The key is to become self-aware of every time you get that divided feeling that is taking your energy away from healing.

# LEVEL 2 – THE RESISTANT PICTURE

Next, check if your resistance has an associated image. It might be an image of you in the future still sick, or a picture from your past where everything was well.

It's probably easy to understand why you might want to use EFT on a future image where everything is not healed. But why would you tap on a past picture when everything was well? Tapping on a picture like this would help you release the emotional pain that is being created currently in your body when you visualise it. It could be a heartache or a longing for what was, for example.

Use the EFT Tapping Protocol to resolve the feelings around the picture, remembering to take a SUDs level before and after the exercise. For example,

> 'Even though I see myself sick in the future, and it creates this heaviness in my chest, I deeply and completely accept myself.'

> 'Even though I remember being well in the past, and it makes me feel heavy and sad, I deeply and completely accept myself.'

Continue until you can visualise each past or future picture from a neutral state.

## LEVEL 3 – PAST COMMENTS AND EVENTS

It may not just be your own fears and insecurities that are driving your resistance. There may have been prior life experiences that are currently reinforcing your resistance to the condition. Things that were said to you by others, either when you were ill on previous occasions or this time around. For some clients, this part can include more stressful life events such as times when they were dumped by friends or relatives because they were sick, for example.

Use the 'Tell the Story' technique to take the emotional charge out of any past memories where you were conditioned to resist your illness. Take them one at a time. Some of these memories might have one single peak, such as a throwaway comment a parent or carer made when you were sick as a child. Others might have several peaks, such as the time when you were fired for repeated sickness. If you are treating a memory with several peaks (in this case it might be your boss's words when he fired you, the look on the faces of the other staff as you left the office, the raised voice of your partner when you got home), remember to tap on the emotional intensity of each peak, identifying where you feel it in your body and tapping until it resolves each time.

## MORE ON SURRENDER

Surrender is the opposite of resistance. Just to reiterate, surrendering to your condition does not mean giving in to being sick. In the *The Healing Game*, surrender plays a very different role. We accept wholeheartedly the current predicament that we find ourselves in *and* we create the circumstances for healing from a place of peace.

This does not mean paying lip service to accepting it, whilst simultaneously resisting it inside. That's why the surrender component of *The Healing Game* has three levels:

· Self-acceptance
· Self-forgiveness
· Self-love

We explored self-love in Chapter 5, but we are going to revisit it in relation to surrender. As we said previously, there is often a huge disparity between the understanding that we need to love ourselves, and the reality of not actually feeling that love. It's another situation in which we can find ourselves divided, saying that we love ourselves whilst quietly boiling away with self-resentment, judgement and blame.

Self-love has two inbuilt components. The first is self-acceptance, and the second is self-forgiveness. When you are fully experiencing self-acceptance and self-forgiveness, then self-love comes more naturally. If you are trying to force self-love whilst simultaneously harbouring a lack of acceptance and forgiveness towards yourself, then self-love will be nothing more than a concept.

## EXERCISE

Revisit the self-love work from Chapter 5.

Have you already cleared your blocks to self-love? Did you break the habits of self-criticism? Are you treating yourself with the same tenderness you would a five-year-old child? Are there any blocks to self-love that you didn't address earlier, and that are more apparent now that you have done some deeper self-work?

## SELF-ACCEPTANCE

What would it take for you to fully accept the condition you find yourself in?

Look deep within at any aspect of the condition and your relationship to it that you don't accept. These can include things that you may have done that could have exacerbated the condition, such as prolonged unsupportive dietary or lifestyle choices. Perhaps you travelled to a foreign country and subsequently got sick, or compromised in a toxic relationship or career choice, until your body broke down. With the hindsight of what you know now, you could have made different life choices, but the key is to find peace with whatever you did or didn't do, as part of the healing process.

## *Rachel* – CHRONIC PAIN, NEUROPATHY

Rachel worked in a demanding law firm. She wanted to prove to her family that she could be successful. She pushed and demanded more of herself, even when in pain and exhausted. Eventually she was forced to stop working. Rachel was angry with herself and her body. We tapped on a whole host of issues – not only her anger, but the reasons behind why she pushed herself so hard. There was a deep, overriding urge to compare herself to her sister's success. After we worked together, she had a greater level of acceptance and understanding of why she'd done what she'd done.

## EXERCISE

In your journal, write one of the following statements at the top of each page:
- I should have . . .
- I shouldn't have . . .

Then make a list under each, without thinking too much about it. Although this exercise is designed to highlight the specific ways in which you may blame yourself for your current condition, it may highlight some other areas in your life where you are subconsciously playing the shame or blame game.

You might end up with a list of statements. If any of those statements have emotional intensity that shows up in your body, you have material for tapping. Tapping on the statements, whilst identifying the area in the body where you feel the intensity, will help you create perceptual shifts and release the energetic charge around each statement.

For example: 'Even though I have all this guilt in my stomach for pushing myself before I got sick, I deeply and completely accept myself.'

You may want to go deeper than simply creating a perceptual shift. If you have specific memories that relate to any guilt, shame or blame you are harbouring, you can use the 'Tell the Story' technique to take the charge out of each specific peak.

## SELF-FORGIVENESS

The second layer of surrendering to where you are is forgiving yourself for all that has gone before. When the first layer of self-acceptance has been experienced, and the underlying shame and blame are no longer the predominant emotions, there is room for other emotions, such as compassion, to be experienced.

Once you have completed the first exercise on self-acceptance, you may find that you start to see your situation more from an outside perspective and less from behind the filters of your perception. Some thoughts that you may find yourself thinking include:

- I can see I did my best with the knowledge and wisdom I had at the time
- I've grown so much from that event and I wouldn't be who I am today without it

From this viewpoint, you may begin to accept that you made certain mistakes in life in order to grow.

## *Ruth* – Terminal Bowel Cancer

Ruth was very angry towards herself for not accomplishing enough in her life. She felt she had not travelled enough, and not spent enough time with her children – not told them what she needed to express. Through EFT she was able to observe what she'd accomplished in her life, the depth of her relationship with her children, instil an amount of peace around who she was, and see that she'd done her best.

This stage cannot be forced. Take your time and if you need a little extra help, use the EFT Tapping Protocol to explore any blocks you encounter.

## EXERCISE

Now write in your journal: 'I can't forgive myself because . . .'

You may find that different or deeper answers emerge than from the initial 'I should/I shouldn't' exercise. If this is the case, use the EFT Tapping Protocol to either tap on the statements, or go deeper to resolve the memories with the 'Tell the Story' technique, remembering to tap on each peak.

## SELF-LOVE

The more you have cleared the obstacles to self-love with forgiveness and acceptance, the more space you will make for self-love. The two exercises that preceded this may have been sufficient, particularly if carried out thoroughly, and your perception may have already shifted. But if you have been consistently withholding love from yourself, then your self-love may need a little more work, and perhaps even the expert guidance of an EFT practitioner.

## EXERCISE

If you feel equipped to go deeper on your own, write at the top of the next page on your journal: 'I can't love myself because . . .'

Chances are this will highlight even deeper areas to work on, perhaps taking you into some core belief work about worthiness and the belief that you are flawed in some way. If these have a strong or overwhelming charge to them, definitely don't tackle them alone. But if they are mild to moderate, then work with any associated memories or events using the 'Tell the Story' technique.

## GOING DEEPER ON THE SET-UP PHRASE

So far, the set-up phrase we have been using in this book is 'I deeply and completely accept myself.' In conventional EFT, the set-up phrase that is often used is, 'I deeply and completely love and accept myself.' At this stage you may be ready to add this in. Try adding it in, and see how you feel.

## BEING VIGILANT WITH YOUR SELF-TALK

You've probably heard it a thousand times before, but let's not discount the more conventional ways that you can be kind to yourself. Your self-talk will probably begin to naturally change, the more clearing that you do. But be sure that you are not still using the old habits of putting yourself down, being unkind to yourself, or punishing yourself. If you find yourself doing any of these things, pause, tap on the emotion that has come up, and then practice being extremely kind to yourself. Remember, you ideally want to speak to yourself with the kindness that you would use when speaking to a small child. It can take a while for this to become habitual, particularly if you have been unkind to yourself for some time.

## TIME FOR A VOC CHECK

Out of 100 per cent, how resistant are you to your condition now? Or, we could look from a new perspective and ask: Out of 100 per cent, how much am I experiencing peace and surrender around my current condition (100 being total peace, and 0 being zero peace)? Remember that this has nothing to do with powerlessness or giving into the condition. Instead, it is allowing yourself the valuable, guilt-free rest you may need in order for your body to recover.

Now that we've hopefully got you to a state of more peace and relaxation with your state of well-being (with the understanding that this is a dynamic, ongoing process), in the next chapter we'll explore taking action from a place of greater inner peace.

# CHAPTER TWELVE

# Component 9
# TAKING ACTION

S O FAR, MUCH OF WHAT WE HAVE DONE is to transform your inner climate. Hopefully, you now have a much better understanding of your inner world as a result, and no longer feel at the mercy of your emotions or your current condition. If you have been consistently applying the exercises in this book, or working with a practitioner to support your healing, you have likely found that some of your filters, beliefs and programmes about healing have begun to transform radically.

However, although we have been paying careful attention to your healing on an emotional/energetic plane, we want to ensure that you are also addressing any action that you need to take in your external reality, to continue to support your inner healing.

In this chapter we are going to address all the other components that will reinforce the work that we have been doing together.

## DIET

There is a plethora of diet books and it is far beyond the scope of this book to suggest any dietary advice. First and foremost, diet is a very personal thing, and there are often considerations specific to individual conditions. However, at the same time, I don't want to pretend that just tapping and then ignoring what you put in your body is going to have the same impact as tapping *and* paying attention to what supports your healing and what drains it.

There are two levels on which we can address diet. They are: increasing your awareness of what actually works for you and contributes to your healing, and what takes from you and detracts from your state of healing.

For example, one of my clients with Crohn's disease worked through *The Healing Game* at the same time as she committed herself to the GAP diet (Gut and Psychology Diet). She felt that the two approaches dynamically supported each other, and the effectiveness of each one on its own became heightened when it was joined with the other. Other clients have also had success with the Paleo Diet, Specific Carbohydrate Diet, gluten- and lactose-free diets, and so on.

A further extension of this is that often I hear clients say something along the lines of: 'Food is my only comfort when I am sick. I have given up everything else. I don't see why I should give this up.' Some clients feel totally deprived on their specialised diets, and this can lead to a feeling of loss. This can be tapped on as well.

If the charge on this is strong for you, try the following tapping statement, addressing one issue at a time. Remember to notice where you feel the disruption in your physical body:

'Even though I don't want to let go of wheat/sugar/ coffee/alcohol, and this is standing in the way of my healing, I deeply and completely accept myself.'

You can also tap on your specific attachments and cravings as they come up:

'Even though I really want this pasta, I deeply and completely accept myself.'

Furthermore, you can clear the underlying emotional factors that you may be using food to block. Many of us in the West were trained to believe that food is love. If you have deep and complex issues related to this, then it is best to work through them with a practitioner. If your issues aren't too deeply rooted, you can begin with this tapping statement and see where it leads you:

'Even though I was taught by my _____ (relative) that food is love, I deeply and completely accept myself.'

Another component, which is less widely understood, is that there may be a part of you that feels it doesn't deserve to have good, nutritious, healing foods. If you worked through the unworthiness and self-worth exercises in Chapter 5, this will have probably cleared by now. If not, consider the following tapping statement. If it holds any charge for you, use the EFT Tapping Protocol until it dissolves.

'Even though I feel I don't deserve to nourish myself, I deeply and completely accept myself.'

Also consider that this may bring up some further memories to resolve around poverty, worthiness, lack, and so on. Use the 'Tell the Story' technique if earlier memories are triggered.

## PHYSICAL EXERCISE

Just as for diet, recommendations for exercise are condition-specific. When I was recovering from chronic fatigue syndrome, graded exercise was recommended, and this type of gradual reintroduction of physical activity (obviously under the recommendation of your physician), can be helpful for many conditions. Moving your body in a way that doesn't cause too much strain is a vital recommendation. Exercise will alter your mental state, and your psychology will follow your physiology. When you are sick, especially if you have been bed-ridden for a long time, as I was, there is a tremendous amount of strain on the blood vessels and the whole energy system. Beginning to move is going to change your energy levels, your psychology, your perception and your overall state of well-being. I started doing bed yoga each morning, and then gradually used gentle yoga, as well as T'ai Chi, as I got stronger.

You can use the EFT Tapping Protocol to tap on any resistance you have to starting to move again, using the following, or similar, set-up statement.

'Even though I have all this resistance to moving my body, I deeply and completely accept myself.'

You may also have some fear around overdoing it that prevents you from exercising at all. I didn't start doing real physical exercise until years after my illness because I was afraid of relapsing, even though I knew of the benefits of exercise. You could use a set-up statement such as:

'Even though I'm afraid to exercise, in case I push myself too far, I deeply and completely accept myself.'

## ENVIRONMENT

What is the world immediately around you like? Does it contribute to your healing or drain it? Are there things in the house that have old associations and connections for you?

First of all, things in your environment could hold clues to unresolved issues that you have. Look around the room that you are in right now. Does anything trigger a strong reaction or resistance in you? How about a sinking in your heart or a painful memory? Or maybe an old energy around a conflict or separation? If any object triggers you, you can obviously get rid of it. However, if you want to clear the meaning and significance you have placed upon it, you can place it in front of you, start to tap, and work through any triggers, emotions or memories that it creates.

Most likely, if an object catches your eye a number of times throughout the day, it will have been subtly draining you.

There are other considerations that are beyond the scope of this book, such as environmental toxins, electromagnetic fields (EMFs), and pollutants that might be affecting your healing. Again, a detailed analysis of these is way beyond what I can offer here. There are obvious things that you can do to support the energy work we are doing together, such as turning off the Wi-Fi at night, ensuring that you only spend short periods each day on computers and electrical equipment, and so on. You can also learn a practice called Earthing where you lie on the bare ground for 20 minutes per day. This practice is said to have tremendous effects on physical healing and will dramatically support your EFT and other practices.

## RELATIONSHIPS

Are there any relationships that are consistently triggering or draining you? Many times we become accustomed to compromising in relationships (either romantic, family, work or friendship). It is a socially acceptable part of our human conditioning.

Often, we don't say anything because we don't want to rock the boat. When you are recovering from a long-term illness, you don't necessarily have the luxury of compromising on that which drains you. It is recommended that you reserve every bit of energy for healing.

This component has several aspects to it. If you are constantly getting triggered by someone, the first question to ask, without judgement or blame for either person involved, is: 'Is this my stuff, their stuff, or a mixture of both?'

The great thing about having a tool such as EFT at your disposal is, even if it feels like it is 'their stuff', when you clear your side of things, and take responsibility (without blame) for what is coming up for you, often the way they behave towards you changes too. If you have big challenges with people, try clearing everything this brings up for you (without hoping that it will change them) and see what happens in the process.

When I owned that I was responsible for my relationship as much as my husband was, a lot shifted for me. I addressed why I felt unheard, why I was so angry, and why we were unable to communicate. I had wanted my husband to change and I was angry with him because he didn't. Once my perspective shifted, he was different too.

### *Caroline* - LYME DISEASE

Caroline's husband had been her 'knight in shining armour' when she was first diagnosed with Lyme disease. As the condition progressed, it started to take its toll on their relationship and they had separated.

We used EFT to work through the beliefs that were preventing her from living a full life, and supporting herself.

Another aspect to this is that you might find yourself in a particular role with certain people in your life. Other people's projections and expectations about who you are and your ability to heal can have a detrimental effect on your healing. I've witnessed parents who have an over-mothering quality, and appear to almost enjoy having a sick child, because it gives them a sense of purpose or a way of showing love, and an opportunity to show complete dedication to the child. This kind of behaviour does not usually take place on a conscious level, and often there is a lack of awareness around what is going on, on the part of one or both parties.

Sometimes, there are more overt comments from friends or family members that can trigger you, too. Just as you did when clearing your environment to make room for your healing, you may also have to move on from some destructive relationships as you heal. Some of my clients have had to take extreme measures, such as space from family members, in order to create a favourable social environment in which to heal.

Another aspect that I have observed is a friendship that was made on your healing journey with someone who has the same condition as you. If this is a transformational friendship and you share the goal of you both healing, then this can be highly evolutionary for you both. However, be aware of any friendship that you have formed that is reinforcing the condition. If you are spending time with someone who is healing the same condition as you, they will be in a similar energetic frequency as that which you are experiencing. In order to heal, you want to ensure that you are changing your energetic frequency and not reinforcing it. Spending time with other healthy, optimistic and positive people is also a vital part of the process of you healing your condition.

## JOY, LAUGHTER AND FUN

Healing can feel like a very serious business! Throughout this book I have challenged you to go deep on your unresolved emotional challenges and to look at some parts of yourself that you may have been squashing down. Hopefully we have done so in as light and fun a way as possible. I also want to ensure that you are backing this up with other experiences that connect you with the joy of living. This is *The Healing Game*, after all, and I want to ensure you are playing it, and not simply dragging yourself from clearing to clearing with no fun in the middle.

Do something joyful every day and laugh every day. You might need comedy to help you, and if this is the case, ensure that you have an arsenal of clips lined up on YouTube. You may even want to go further and explore a practice such as laughter yoga, which also dramatically increases endorphins and is said to improve healing. Whatever practice you choose, ensure that you engage in something consistently that makes your heart sing. Play your favourite music, and if you're able to, dance! Spend time with your pets, too. So many of my clients tell me they couldn't have got through the illness if it hadn't been for their dog or cat. Tap on any resistance you might have to having fun:

'Even though I've been resisting joy and fun, I deeply and completely accept myself.'

'Even though I haven't been valuing myself enough to have fun, I deeply and completely accept myself.'

If you consistently apply these changes in your external reality, the inner work that you have been doing will be matched by your outer world.

# CONCLUSION

A T THIS POINT, you have either skimmed this book through and are about to embark on the journey, or you have dived right in and undertaken a number of the exercises on a daily basis. If you are at the former stage, I want to invite you to delve in deeply and go for it. And if you are already on this journey with me, I want to sincerely congratulate you for the courage I know that it takes.

I highlighted at the start of this book that, although I could not guarantee your physical healing, if you undertook the exercises in this book, something would change. Hopefully by now you have, at least, a clearer understanding of why you may have got sick, and tools to transform whatever you found beneath the surface.

You still might have a way to go. There is always that point when we are halfway up a mountain and it still looks like such a long way to the top. It is often not easy for us to give ourselves credit for how far we have climbed. I often say to clients that it can take years of stress, negatively impacting core beliefs, distorted perceptions and programmed points of view to make the body sick. The EFT tools we have worked with have the ability to powerfully undo that which has gone before. And they have the ability to help you remember who you truly are beyond your conditioning and your patterns. Some things can take a while to undo, so I want to encourage you to be patient as the remainder of your journey unfolds. Go back through the exercises. Dig deeper. Sometimes on the second or third time around, you will discover a gem that is at the core and the whole thing will unfold. At one moment you can have a dark night of the soul and believe that the journey will be never-ending. Two days later you can have found the linch-pin that was at the core of your belief system, and your whole world can shift 180 degrees.

## SUMMARY OF THE COMPONENTS

Below, look over the 9 components of *The Healing Game* once again. As you do, ask yourself:
- Are there any components that I missed or skimmed over?
- Is there anywhere I could go deeper?
- With what I know now, and after clearing and shifting so much, are there any components I could revisit to get a deeper perspective?

## PART A – THE TRIGGER

SYMPTOMS – Revisit what was happening in your life on the run-up to the appearance of the symptoms. Does it have the same charge when you think about it now? Are there any aspects that you missed or didn't consider the first time around?

SATISFACTION – How satisfied were you with your life when the symptoms appeared? How do you relate to the question of life satisfaction now? Are you clearer on your purpose and how you are going to move forward with it? Does thinking about your life purpose fill you with dread or joy? Is there still more work to do on this, so that you know what your purpose is and are on track with it?

SHOWING UP – How were you showing up in your life on the run-up to the appearance of the symptoms? How does that compare to how you are showing up in your life right now, after you have done so much clearing?

## PART B – THE CONNECTOR

THE GATEWAY – Who are you beyond your triggers, beliefs and programmes? This question should be much easier for you to answer now. Have you got a clearer sense that your triggers and programmes aren't you? That there is a you beyond your life experiences and the triggers they created for you?

WHY CAN'T I . . . ? – What's been preventing you from showing up in your life as your true, authentic self? Have you got a clearer idea of this now, and tackled it at the root?

WHAT WOULD HAPPEN IF . . . ? – What would your life be like if you showed up as your true, authentic self all of the time? How is your authenticity these days? Do you find you are ready to bring more of yourself to the world and remove your mask? Are there any areas of your life where you could do this more?

## PART C – THE TRANSFORMER

ADDRESSING THE FEAR – What fears do you have about healing? Have you addressed all your underlying fears so that you are able to heal more freely?

SURRENDERING – What would it take for you to fully accept the condition you find yourself in? Have you been able to surrender, yet still take action towards healing at the same time?

TAKING ACTION – What action do you need to take in your external world to create the ideal conditions for healing? Have you been taking that action on all levels? What have you noticed as a result?

For me, healing my condition was really the start of my life. I stepped out into a whole new world after I had healed physically. The emotional healing continued to happen after the physical body had healed. There was a tipping point where the emotions no longer had such a detrimental effect on my body. Where I could function again. But the journey did not stop there. There are always deeper layers of self-love. The more I peeled back, the more I could operate more effectively in the world, and the more people I could help accordingly. Writing this book was yet another one of those layers. I'm sure there will be more to come! I also want to thank you sincerely for being part of this journey with me. I look forward to hearing about your successes and your own healing as you play *The Healing Game*.

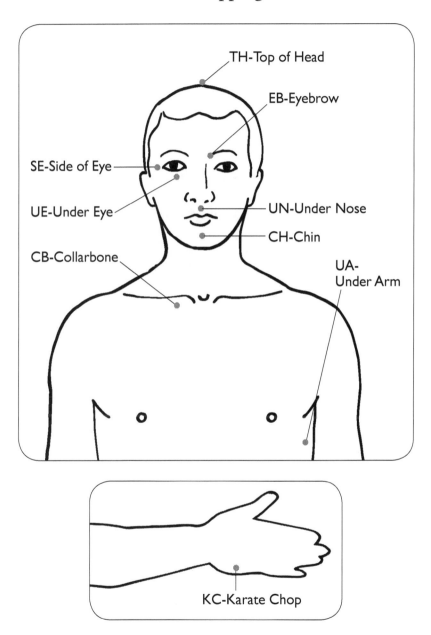

TH-Top of Head

EB-Eyebrow

SE-Side of Eye

UE-Under Eye

UN-Under Nose

CH-Chin

CB-Collarbone

UA-
Under Arm

KC-Karate Chop

## EFT QUICK START

Bring to mind the past memory (a single event with a single trigger) that you want to work on.

### Step One – Identify the Feeling and its Location

What are you feeling and where are you feeling it in your body?

The feeling can be an emotion, such as sadness, fear, isolation, panic, rage, embarrassment, terror, and so on. The feeling also usually shows up somewhere in the body, for example, the stomach, the heart, the chest, and so on.

### Step Two – Give it a Score Out of Ten

Once you have determined what you are feeling and where you are feeling it in your body, it's time to give it a 'SUDs' level. In EFT, SUDs stands for 'Subjective Unit of Distress'. It's the scale that is used to measure how intense the issue is for you in the current moment – 1 being barely there at all and 10 being overwhelming. The reason you take this measurement at the start is that it helps you to see your progress when you apply the EFT Tapping Protocol. The thing to remember about the SUDs level is that it is how you feel in the current moment when you think about it, and not how you felt at the time.

## Step Three – The Set-Up Phrase

The feeling and its location are used to form the set-up statement.

'Even though I have this _____ (feeling) in my _____ (location), I deeply and completely accept myself.'

For example: 'Even though I have this rage in my heart, I deeply and completely accept myself.'

As an alternative to 'I deeply and completely accept myself,' you can use one of the following to create the latter half of your set-up statement:

· 'I accept all of me.'

· 'I accept who I am and how I'm feeling.'

· 'I want to accept myself.'

· 'I'm open to the possibility I could accept myself.'

Tapping on the side of either one of your hands, using the fingertips of your opposite hand, say the set-up statement out loud three times.

### Step Four – The Reminder Phrase

Now shorten the set-up statement to a reminder phrase. The reminder phrase is what you are feeling and where you are feeling it in your body.
For example: This rage in my heart.

### Step Five – The Tapping Protocol

Repeat the reminder phrase each time you tap on the following points with your first two fingers, on either side of the body:

- **Top of your head** - right on the crown
- **Eyebrow** - where your eyebrow starts
- **Side of the eye** - on the eye socket bone, at outside of each eye
- **Under your eye** - on the eye socket bone, an inch under the pupil
- **Under your nose** - in the dent which is above your lip
- **Chin** - on the crease of your chin
- **On the collarbone** - if you go out diagonally an inch from where a gentleman would have his tie knot, there is a slight hollow there
- **Under the arm** - for the gentleman, in line with the nipple and for the lady, in line with the bra strap

## Step Six – Repeat Several Rounds

Practice tapping on the points for 3 or 4 rounds so that you get used to them, while repeating your reminder phrase. (Later you will learn to vary the reminder phrase, but at this stage say the same one over and over again, to keep it simple.)

## Step Seven – Recheck the SUDs Level (Score Out of 10)

Now check if anything has changed. Does the original trigger have the same impact on you? Has the SUDs level gone down? If it has, then great, you have had your first experience of using EFT on yourself. If you didn't get a result or it went up, don't be discouraged. You may have picked a memory that has more than one aspect (such as the tone of your teacher's voice and the look on their face as they scolded you, for example).

## APPENDIX 3: 'Tell the Story' Technique

If you have a memory that you feel able to work with and handle on your own, make sure it is a small-t trauma and a single event. It needs to be something that happened in a short space of time, such as a few minutes. If it spans several hours, days or weeks, break it up into a number of smaller events, all with their own beginning, middle and end.

### Step One – The Title

Give the memory you have chosen a title, such as 'The Worst Day of My Life.' The reason that we give it a title is that we can take the SUDs level (the score out of 10) on what emotions the title evokes in you, and take some of the charge out of the memory generally before we get into the specific aspects.

### Step Two – Adapting the Set-Up Phrase

Now create the set-up phrase. This time we are going to adapt it to fit the exercise:

'Even though I have this _____ (feeling + location) when I think of _____ (title), I deeply and completely accept myself.'

Example: 'Even though I have this fear in my heart when I think of The Worst Day of My Life, I deeply and completely accept myself.'

Tap on the karate chop point and repeat 3 times.

**Step Three – Reminder Phrase**

Now start to tap around the points. This time you can mix your reminder phrase up a little bit so that you aren't saying the same thing every time. For example:

- **Tapping on the top of the head** – this fear in my heart
- **Tapping on the eyebrow** – the worst day of my life
- **Tapping on the side of the eye** – this fear in my heart
- **Tapping under your eye** – it was the worst day I ever had
- **Tapping under your nose** – this fear
- **Tapping on the chin** – the worst day
- **Tapping on the collarbone** – this fear in my heart
- **Tapping under the arm** – the worst day of my life

Continue until the SUDs on the title is down to a 3 or less (you may not clear it all the first time you use this technique, as aspects that occur later in the story may need to be dealt with before the title is a zero).

### Step Four – Tell the Story Out Loud

Now, start telling the story to yourself *out loud*. You are going to need to be very self-aware at this stage, because the second that an aspect of the story raises your emotional intensity, you are going to tap on it using the EFT Tapping Protocol. We are literally breaking the story down into one trigger at a time. Look for what you:

- Saw
- Heard
- Felt
- Smelt
- Tasted

Each one of these could be a separate trigger.

### Step Five - Tap on Each Trigger Individually

At each point you come to a trigger, adapt the set-up statement to fit the experience, and tap on it until the SUDs level is a zero. Here are some examples of adapted set-up statements for the different senses:

Set-Up Phrase: 'Even though she looked so angry and it gives me this sinking feeling in my chest, I deeply and completely accept myself.'

(Reminder Phrases - alternating between: she looked so angry / this sinking feeling in my chest)

Set-Up Phrase: 'Even though I can still hear him yelling, and I have a ringing in my ears, I deeply and completely accept myself.'

(Reminder Phrases - alternating between: his yelling/ this ringing in my ears)

Set-Up Phrase: 'Even though she slapped me and it makes my throat tighten with sadness, I deeply and completely accept myself.'

(Reminder Phrases - alternating between: slapped me/this tightening throat/this sadness in my throat)

Set-Up Phrase: 'Even though I can still smell the burning, and it fills my heart with fear, I deeply and completely accept myself.'

(Reminder Phrases - alternating between: the smell of burning/this fear in my heart)

Set-Up Phrase: 'Even though I can still taste the fumes, and it causes a gagging in my throat, I deeply and completely accept myself.'

(**Reminder Phrases – alternating between:** tasting the fumes/this gagging in my throat)
Continue through the memory, clearing each trigger until it is a zero.

## Step Six – Retell the Story Out Loud

At the end, test the original title, and see if there is any charge remaining. Then tell the story again, to check that you have resolved all the aspects. There may be parts that you missed that you need to go back over until the whole memory is a zero.

## APPENDIX 4: Personal Peace Procedure

Earlier in this book we highlighted how the conventional Personal Peace Procedure, created by Gary Craig, is a popular way to clear your past trauma in the world of EFT. It involves making a list of all your 'small-t' and 'big-T' memories and literally working through them one by one for 365 days.

Whilst this is a very effective and powerful practice, I suggest a slightly different way of approaching your personal work. While I recommend working on a memory a day (minimum) when healing long-term illness, I would work on the ones that are most relevant to your current situation.

Look at what is not working in your life right now: relationships, finances, and of course health. Pick one topic at a time. Start to tap as you close your eyes, and ask for a relevant memory to surface. Once you have one, you can carry out the 'Tell the Story' Technique. Doing this every day with commitment will likely have an effect on both your emotional and physical health.

# APPENDIX 5: Clinical Research on EFT

The following is a clinical study carried out on the effectiveness of EFT for the treatment of emotional conditions.

Stewart A, Boath E, Carryer A, Walton I, Hill L. *Can Emotional Freedom Techniques (EFT) be effective in the treatment of emotional conditions? Results of a service evaluation in Sandwell.* Journal of Psychological Therapies in Primary Care 2013; 2:71-84.

## ABSTRACT

**Objectives:** This service evaluation (pilot study) was carried out to establish the feasibility and effectiveness of Emotional Freedom Techniques (EFT) within a healthcare setting. A dedicated EFT service was delivered in a community setting within the National Health Service in the Metropolitan Borough of Sandwell, United Kingdom.

**Method:** Over a 13-month period, clients accessing the service for a range of emotional conditions were studied. All referrals came through a centralised hub; clients could also self-refer and referrals were accepted for any condition, providing that clients were aged over 18, and not classed as "vulnerable adults". At the start and end of their treatment, clients were asked to complete the CORE-10 scale (psychological distress; main outcome variable), Warwick-Edinburgh Mental Well-Being Scale (WEMWBS; mental well-being),

Rosenberg Self-Esteem and Hospital Anxiety and Depression Scale (HADS; anxiety and depression) measurement scales.

**Results:** Thirty-nine clients gave consent. The main presenting conditions were anxiety (23; 59.0%), depression (5; 12.8%), and anger (4; 10.3%). The mean number of sessions attended was 5.05 (median 4.0; range 2-17). At the end of therapy, there were both statistically and clinically significant improvements for CORE-10 (Pre-therapy=20.16; Post-therapy=8.71; SD=6.81; p < .001; n=38), WEMWBS (Pre-therapy=38.27; Post-therapy=53.62; SD=10.88; p < .001; n=37), Rosenberg Self-Esteem (Pre-therapy=14.16; Post-therapy=21.81; SD=6.88; p < .001; n=31), HADS Anxiety (Pre-therapy=13.22 ; Post-therapy=7.30 ; SD=3.57; p < .001; n=23), HADS Depression (Pre-therapy=9.26 ; Post-therapy=4.87; SD=5.25; p = .001; n=23) and HADS total score (Pre-therapy=22.30; Post-therapy=12.13; SD=8.17; p < .001; n=23). All but one of the clients showed clinical improvements. Few clients attended for follow-up at three months post-therapy, but clinical significance was retained for those clients, with statistical significance for pre-therapy-follow-up for CORE-10 (Pre-therapy=18.71; Follow-up=7.14; SD= 6.37; p= .003; n=7), WEMWBS (Pre-therapy=40.00; Follow-up=53.29; SD=11.27; p= .021; n=7), Rosenberg Self-Esteem (Pre-therapy=14.29; Follow-up=22.43; SD=6.45; p= .016; n=7) and HADS Depression (Pre-therapy=8.50; Follow-up=2.75; SD=2.50; p = .019; n=4).

**Conclusions:** Despite limitations, the results support the potential of EFT as an effective treatment for a range of psychological and physical disorders. As an average of just over 5 sessions were required, it is possible that EFT may also be very cost-effective. Further, larger studies are required, which may provide definitive evidence of its effectiveness.

Boath, E.H, Stewart, T and Carryer A. (2012) *A narrative systematic review of the effectiveness of Emotional Freedom Techniques (EFT).* Staffordshire University, CPSI Monograph.

## ABSTRACT

EFT (Emotional Freedom Techniques) is a new and emerging energy psychology. This narrative systematic review aimed to identify and assess the quality of all published randomised controlled trials (RCTs) of EFT in order to: evaluate the effectiveness of EFT in treating a range of psychological disorders and to compare the effectiveness of EFT with other interventions used for treating those disorders.

**Methodology:** A literature search was carried out of CINAHL, Cochrane Library, MEDLINE, PsycINFO, PsychARTICLES, Proquest, PubMED, Sciencedirect, SPORTdiscus, Swetswise, Web of Knowledge, Web of Science and ZETOC, using the key terms EFT and energy psychology. Calls for published, unpublished and ongoing RCTs of EFT were sent to Newsletters and to the Association of Energy Psychology and the Foundation for Epigenetic Medicine. Contact was made with researchers and practitioners in the field. Conference proceedings and reference lists of retrieved articles were hand searched. Abstracts of articles were reviewed and full copies acquired if the title and/or abstract identified the paper as an RCT of EFT. Two authors independently rated and assessed the quality of each trial using the Critical Appraisal Skills Programme (CASP) for randomised controlled trials and the Jadad Scale.

Results: The search strategy identified a total of 42 published studies of EFT. Seven RCTs of EFT were included. Methodological flaws in the studies are highlighted and discussed. EFT was shown to be effective in treating Post-Traumatic Stress Disorder (PTSD), Fibromyalgia, Phobias, test anxiety and athletic performance. EFT was shown to be superior to diaphragmatic breathing (DB), Progressive Muscular Relaxation (PMR), an inspirational lecture and a Support Group. Only Eye Movement, Desensitization and Reprocessing (EMDR) was superior to EFT. EFT may be an efficient and effective intervention for a range of psychological disorders. Given the methodological limitation of these RCTs, further good quality research on EFT is warranted.

# Bibliography

Braden, Gregg, *The Divine Matrix,* Hay House, 2008

Brown, Brene, *Daring Greatly: How the Courage to Be Vulnerable Transforms the Way We Live, Love, Parent, and Lead,* Gotham Books, 2012

Brown, Brene, *I Thought It Was Just Me (But It Isn't): Making the Journey from 'What Will People Think?' to 'I Am Enough',* Gotham Books, 2007

Church, Dawson, *The Genie in your Genes: Epigenetic Medicine and the New Biology of Intention,* Energy Psychology Press, 2009

Craig, Gary, *The EFT Manual,* Elite Books, 2011

Dawson, Karl and Marilatt, K., *Transform Your Beliefs, Transform Your Life: EFT Tapping Using Matrix Reimprinting,* Hay House UK, 2014

Dawson, Karl and Allenby, S., *Matrix Reimprinting Using EFT,* Hay House UK, 2014

Eden, Donna, *Energy Medicine,* Jeremy P Tarcher/Penguin, 1999

Flook, Richard, *Why Am I Sick? How to Find Out What's Really Wrong Using Advanced Clearing Energetics,* Hay House, 2013

Hass, Rue, *Emotional Freedom Techniques for the Highly Sensitive Temperament,* Energy Psychology Press, 2009

Hay, Louise, *You Can Heal Your Life,* Hay House, 1984

Katie, Byron (with Stephen Mitchell), *Loving What Is: Four Questions that Can Change Your Life,* Three Rivers Press, 2002

Levine, Peter A., *Waking the Tiger: Healing Trauma,* New Atlantic Books, 1997

Lipton, Bruce H., *The Biology of Belief: Unleashing the Power of Consciousness, Matter and Miracles,* Hay House, 2011

Mate, Gabor, *When the Body Says No: The Cost of Hidden Stress,* Vintage Canada, 2003

Myss, Caroline, *Anatomy of the Spirit,* Three Rivers Press, 1996

McTaggart, Lynne, *The Field,* Element, 2003

Newbigging, Sandy C., *Thunk! How to Think Less for Serenity and Success,* Findhorn Press, 2012

Newbigging, Sandy C., *Mind Calm,* Hay House, 2014

Ortner, Nick, *The Tapping Solution,* Hay House, 2013

Pert, Candace B., *Molecules of Emotion: Why You Feel the Way You Feel,* Pocket Books, 1999

Richardson, Cheryl, *Take Time for Your Life: A Seven-Step Program for Creating the Life that You Want,* Bantam Books, 2000

Scaer, Robert, *The Body Bears the Burden: Trauma, Dissociation and Disease,* Routledge, 2014

Sheldrake, Rupert, *Morphic Resonance: The Nature of Formative Causation,* Park Street Press, 2009

# Acknowledgements

IT'S SAID THAT EVERYONE HAS A BOOK WITHIN THEM. I've worked in the field of chronic illness since 2004, and early on, I realised there was so much I'd learned from my own illness and from that of my clients. There was so much to write about the subject, yet I lacked the confidence to put pen to paper. This book would not have been possible without the constant support, love and encouragement from so many. So many friends and colleagues held me accountable. Towards the end of 2013, I knew it was now or never − I had to write the book!

Without EFT there would be no book in your hands now. Without Gary Craig, there would be no EFT. I am indebted to the creator of EFT, Gary Craig. He offered a light at the end of a very dark tunnel. He worked with me for hours at a UK EFT Conference for Serious Diseases, and he stayed in touch with me afterwards, checking in on a regular basis.

Thank you to Josephine and George. You weathered the storm of what it meant to be the primary care givers of a 30-year-old who needed her hair washed, meals cooked, cleaning done, groceries bought, and to be told she'd be OK. You put your own lives on hold to care for me. I love you both very much.

Thank you to my dear friends, Sofia da Cunha Reis, Brian and Georgina Johnstone, Sophie St. Pierre, Larisse Goldstein and Maarten Van Nus. Your unconditional support and love warm my heart every day.

A BIG thank you to my soul sisters and brother who had my back for 7 months, and who challenged me when I stopped believing in myself: Gina Best, Kaman Kwok, Anne Beaulieu,

Rhiannon Foster and James L.J. Hargis. Failure is an important ingredient of my success, but quitting is not.

Thanks to some very special EFT colleagues who have become friends along the way: Gail Mae Ferguson, Ingrid Dinter, Liesel Teversham, Uli Mueller, Bernadette Hunter, and Sherry Lukey. I am so very grateful to you all.

Deep appreciation to the Number One man in my life. Michael, we have weathered many storms together. We've laughed our heads off, and cried our hearts out. Thank you for believing in me and never, ever, losing sight of the bigger picture. I love you deeply.

To Jackie McDonald, a young woman who is a most amazing role model to Mirra. Thank you for allowing me to mentor you last year.

Gratitude to some very special clients: Sarah Vanderheiden, Annette Filmer Landers, Kyla Maki, Merle Hindley, Sandra Simmons, Evan and Anna Booher. You are examples of what it means to be fully committed to your health and well-being. It has been my honour to serve you over the years.

Thank you to three leaders who have consistently held a greater vision of me than I could have ever held of myself: Paul Zelizer, thank you for your gentle wisdom, love and support over the years; Dov Baron, thank you for seeing me, believing in me, and knowing I'd rock it, and Sasha Allenby, thank you for knowing exactly what needed to be said, and for making the concept the reality. I am deeply blessed that all three of you walked into my life at exactly the right moment.

Special thanks to Karl Dawson, creator of Matrix Reimprinting, for your ongoing support of me as a Matrix Practitioner and

Trainer, for always making time to talk, and for writing the foreword to this book.

Thanks to Professor Antony Stewart and Dr Elizabeth Hardie Boath for your clinical research.

Thanks to Lois Rose for editing this book, and for your support and enthusiasm.

Thanks to Ann Lowe for the truly beautiful, and inspired, book cover.

A huge thank you to the following for your contribution to the endorsement of this book:

Sasha Allenby, Sharon King, Liesel Teversham, Ingrid Dinter, Jade Barbee, Christian Guenette, Dov Baron, Lindsay Kenny, Paul Zelizer, Sarah Vanderheiden, Dr Elizabeth Boath, Eleanore Duyndam, Mary Llewellyn, Professor Tony Stewart.

# About the Author

ANNABEL FISHER has worked with thousands of chronically ill clients from around the world since 2004. Her journey with this work began when she healed a chronic health condition for which she was wheelchair-bound.

One of Annabel's key strengths when working with others is that she is deeply intuitive. She is able to quickly identify the root cause of an issue with her clients, and help them quickly shift their perspective.

Annabel is the Founder and Creator of The Healing Game Process and the leading authority on using this process to reclaim vibrant health and true authenticity. She is also the host of the internet radio show, *The Healing Game*.

Annabel is a Master Trainer and facilitates EFT and Matrix Reimprinting workshops and training courses worldwide. As well as training others in recognised qualifications, she developed her own rigorous Practitioner Certification Programme.

Annabel has mentored hundreds of new and struggling EFT practitioners to build successful businesses. For almost two years, she was the host of the popular internet radio show, *How to Create a Wildly Successful EFT Practice*. For five years, Annabel organised and hosted the annual Canadian EFT Gathering; she is a inspirational speaker.

To contact Annabel visit:

**www.AnnabelFisher.com**

To deepen your understanding of *The Healing Game,* I'd love you to receive my 3-part video training. You'll hear my insights and benefit from tapping along with me.

Please visit
**www.thehealinggamebook.com**

Made in the USA
Middletown, DE
06 February 2021